THE
MYSTERY
WRITERS
OF
AMERICA
COOKBOOK

Library of Congress Cataloging in
Publication Number: 2014941356

ISBN: 978-1-59474-757-1

Printed in Singapore

Designed by Amanda Richmond
Photography by Steve Legato
Production management by John J. McGurk
Food styling by Ricardo Jattan
Prop styling by Mariellen Melker

Quirk Books
215 Church Street
Philadelphia, PA 19106
quirkbooks.com

10 9 8 7 6 5 4 3 2 1

THE
MYSTERY
WRITERS
OF
AMERICA
COOKBOOK

EDITED BY KATE WHITE

QUIRK BOOKS
PHILADELPHIA

CONTENTS

FEATURING ALL THE USUAL SUSPECTS:

Beth Amos
Kathleen Antrim
Connie Archer
Frankie Y. Bailey
Adrienne Barbeau
Raymond Benson
Karna Small
   Bodman
Rhys Bowen
Susan M. Boyer
Sandra Brown
Leslie Budewitz
Carole Buggé
Lucy Burdette
Alafair Burke
Lorenzo
   Carcaterra
Richard Castle
Diana Chambers
Joelle
   Charbonneau
Lee Child
Laura Childs
C. Hope Clark
Mary Higgins
   Clark
Mary Jane Clark
Harlan Coben
Nancy J. Cohen
Kate Collins

Max Allan Collins
   and Barbara
   Collins
Sheila Connolly
Thomas H. Cook
Mary Ann
   Corrigan
Catherine Coulter
Diane Mott
   Davidson
Nelson DeMille
Gerald Elias
J. T. Ellison
Dianne Emley
Hallie Ephron
Linda Fairstein
Kim Fay
Lyndsay Faye
Sharon Fiffer
Joseph Finder
Bill Fitzhugh
Gillian Flynn
Felix Francis
Meg Gardiner
Alison Gaylin
Daryl Wood Gerber
Sue Grafton
Chuck Greaves
Beth Groundwater
Karen Harper
Charlaine Harris

Carolyn Hart
Greg Herren
Wendy Hornsby
David Housewright
Peter James
J. A. Jance
Tammy Kaehler
Laurie R. King
Lisa King
Rita Lakin
Lois Lavrisa
Allison Leotta
Laura Lippman
Ken Ludwig
John Lutz
Gayle Lynds
Margaret Maron
Edith Maxwell
William Burton
   McCormick
John McEvoy
Brad Meltzer
David Morrell
Marcia Muller
Alan Orloff
Katherine
   Hall Page
Gigi Pandian
Sara Paretsky
James Patterson
Chris Pavone

Louise Penny
Twist Phelan
Gary Phillips
Cathy Pickens
Bill Pronzini
Deanna Raybourn
Kathy Reichs
Barbara Ross
Laura Joh
   Rowland
S. J. Rozan
Hank Phillippi
   Ryan
Justin Scott
Lisa Scottoline
L. J. Sellers
Karin Slaughter
Linda Stasi
Wendy Corsi Staub
Charles Todd
Scott Turow
Lisa Unger
Lea Wait
Mo Walsh
Kate White
Tina Whittle
Jacqueline
   Winspear
Ben H. Winters
Angela Zeman

INTRODUCTION

IN "LAMB TO THE SLAUGHTER," ROALD DAHL'S WICKEDLY delicious 1953 crime short story, a housewife named Mary Maloney listens one evening in dazed horror as her police detective husband announces that he's leaving her. He doesn't give a reason, but it's clear there's another woman. In a moment of sudden fury, Mary grabs the frozen leg of lamb she had planned to roast for dinner and bashes her husband over the head with it, killing him instantly.

But *now* what? she wonders. She certainly doesn't want to go to the gallows for her crime. So Mary sticks the leg of lamb in the oven and, in order to give herself an alibi, sneaks out the back door and goes food shopping. Once she returns home, she calls the police, reporting that she's found her husband murdered. Soon his fellow detectives descend on the scene to investigate, and they observe that their former colleague has been killed by a blow on the back of the head "administered with a heavy blunt instrument." But there's no sign of it anywhere in the apartment.

Finally the lamb is roasted. Mary takes it from the oven and offers slices to the detectives, who devour it eagerly. To them, she is above suspicion, and they remain stumped by the crime scene. If only, they say, there were a murder weapon to inspect. "Get the weapon, and you've got the man," one of them announces. Unfortunately, they've just eaten it.

This may be the single best culinary plot twist in all of mystery writing. But there are plenty of other fabulous ones, as well as countless scenes that mix food and murder. Authors from Arthur Conan Doyle to Dorothy Sayers to Scott Turow have killed off characters with food or drinks laced with poison. Agatha Christie used poison to fell a character in over half of her mystery novels.

But food isn't used just as a weapon. It defines character. As the nineteenth-century French lawyer and gastronomic essayist Jean Brillat-Savarin stated, "Tell me what you eat and I will tell you what you are." That's especially true for the iconic sleuths in mysteries series. We can't think of Miss Marple without her scones and tea (over the course of 12 novels and 20 short stories, she reportedly drank 143 cups of tea), Kinsey Millhone without her peanut butter and pickle sandwich, Jack Reacher without his pots of coffee, Alex "Coop" Cooper without her Dewar's on the rocks, or Nero Wolfe without the outrageous dishes his personal cook, Fritz, makes for him—such as squabs marinated in cream and creole fritters with cheese sauce.

Considering how intertwined food and murder are in fiction, Mystery Writers of America (MWA) decided that it would be a crime not to celebrate this idea, and thus we've created a cookbook especially for mystery fans. It features more than one hundred recipes from many of the top mystery writers in the world, including Mary Higgins Clark, Harlan Coben, Nelson DeMille, Charlaine Harris, and James Patterson. There's even one from Richard Castle, the fictional mystery author on the ABC show *Castle*.

You'll not only love these recipes, you'll also enjoy reading the background information that each author provides. Certain fare comes straight from the pages of the mysteries you love. Other dishes and drinks are author favorites, sometimes indulged in as a reward for a tough day plotting murder and mayhem on the computer.

You might even decide to sample some of these dishes while you're reading a brand-new crime novel. (A helping of Joseph Finder's apple crumble would be the perfect antidote if you're all alone in the house, night has fallen, and you have just reached a particularly terrifying chapter.)

Creating a new recipe is a bit like a detective attempting to solve a murder. "In both situations, you have to use your powers of deduction and work systematically, taking it one step at a time," says Anne Pleshette Murphy, a psychologist, TV journalist, and former editor of *Good Food Magazine*. "A brilliant chef, like an ingenius detective, uses all of his senses and a few pinches of creativity."

By the way, the proceeds from the sale of this book go to MWA, an organization founded in 1945 that is dedicated to promoting higher regard for crime writing, and recognition and respect for those who write within the genre. Membership is open to the public worldwide. It is MWA that sponsors the annual Edgar Awards, named for Edgar Allan Poe and considered the Academy Awards of mystery writing. Among the many wonderful authors and cooks in this book are Edgar winners, MWA Grand Masters, and past national presidents of MWA.

As Sherlock Holmes once said, "Education never ends, Watson." We offer you dozens of recipes to learn, savor, and share!

CHAPTER ONE

The job is tough. I knew that when I was hired on. Some nights are ~~late~~ long. Last night we had a stakeout, and this morning we have no new facts. What we need is some breakfast.

MODEL 1

ALAFAIR BURKE

Ellie Hatcher's Rum-Soaked Nutella French Toast

Readers of my Ellie Hatcher novels may have noticed that the NYPD detective doesn't cook. She eats, but she doesn't cook. The closest she comes to cooking is ordering takeout or dipping her spoon in an ever-handy jar of Nutella. We also know that Ellie likes to drink. Usually it's Johnnie Walker Black or Rolling Rock, or wine if she's at Otto. When you put all that together, I think Ellie would inhale a plate of Rum-Soaked Nutella French Toast, especially if someone else cooked it. (I'm pretty sure her brother, Jess, has prepared more than a few breakfasts in his time.)

YIELD: 4 SERVINGS

8 to 12 tablespoons Nutella

8 ⅜-inch-thick slices brioche or challah

8 large eggs

3 cups milk

2 tablespoons vanilla extract

2 tablespoons dark rum

4 tablespoons (½ stick) butter, divided

Accompaniments: powdered sugar, maple syrup, whipped cream, sliced bananas or berries, or whatever else you want on top

1. Spread 2 to 3 tablespoons of Nutella on half of the brioche slices and then top each with a second slice, forming sandwiches that are about ³⁄₄ inch thick.

2. In a large bowl whisk together eggs, milk, vanilla, and rum. Pour about ¹⁄₂ inch of liquid into a pie pan, shallow baking dish, or other three-dimensional object capable of holding liquid while you dip bread in it.

3. Add 1 tablespoon of the butter to a nonstick skillet over medium heat.

4. While the butter melts, place one Nutella sandwich in the liquid, let it soak for a few seconds, and then flip sandwich to soak the other side briefly. (The idea here is to coat both sides of the sandwich equally instead of dunking the whole thing.)

5. When butter is melted and hot but not smoking, cook sandwich for 3 minutes per side, or until puffed and golden brown. (If your pan is large enough, you can cook multiple sandwiches at a time.) Transfer cooked French toast to a baking sheet and keep warm in oven. Cook remaining sandwiches in newly melted butter in same manner.

6. Sprinkle French toast with powdered sugar and serve with other accompaniments.

ALAFAIR BURKE is the best-selling author of ten novels, including the thriller *Long Gone* and the Ellie Hatcher series: *212*, *Angel's Tip*, *Dead Connection*, *Never Tell*, and *All Day and a Night*. A former prosecutor, she now teaches criminal law and lives in Manhattan.

MARGARET MARON

Granny Knott's Baked Toast

Dorothy Sayers referred to *Busman's Honeymoon* as "A Love Story with Detective Interruptions." I probably should have subtitled *High Country Fall*, tenth in my Judge Deborah Knott series, "A Detective Story with Culinary Interruptions" because I still get requests for recipes from it, especially Granny Knott's baked toast, a homely dish created out of necessity. All it really is is French toast baked in the oven, but Deborah's grandmother never heard of French toast and she was way too busy to make individual servings or measure anything. She cooked "by guess and by golly." When hens nearly stopped laying in winter, this was her way to stretch the eggs.

   Proportions will vary according to the number of mouths to feed. I usually cut thick (1½ to 2 inch) slices from loaves of bread with some body to it: sourdough and whole wheat work well, and so does Italian bread. You want to approximate the thickness of Texas toast even if it takes two slices of your thinner bread to make it up. This is a very forgiving recipe. If you need to feed a larger crowd, figure 1 to 1½ eggs for every cup of milk and adjust the other ingredients as necessary.

YIELD: 6 SERVINGS

1 cup dark brown sugar, divided

½ cup plus 2 tablespoons (1¼ sticks) unsalted butter, divided

¼ cup honey, maple syrup, or molasses

Enough bread slices to cover the bottom of a 9-by-12-inch casserole dish

3 eggs

2 cups milk

½ teaspoon vanilla extract

1. Reserve 2 tablespoons of the brown sugar for later. Cover the bottom of the casserole dish with a thin layer of the remaining brown sugar.

2. Melt 1 stick of butter, stir in the honey, and drizzle over the brown sugar.

3. Lay the bread over the brown sugar, leaving no spaces between slices. (Tear extra slices into small pieces and fill in the cracks.)

4. Beat eggs, milk, and vanilla together and pour over the bread, completely covering it.

5. Lightly sprinkle the reserved 2 tablespoons brown sugar on top. Melt the remaining ¼ stick butter and drizzle over sugar. Cover with plastic wrap and refrigerate overnight.

6. In the morning, preheat oven to 350°F. Pour off most of the liquid that hasn't been absorbed. Bake for 30 to 35 minutes, until a knife inserted into the center comes out clean. The sugar on the bottom should be caramelized and the top well browned. Serve immediately to six hungry people with links or patties of pork sausage. (Do not ask about carbs or calories!)

Winner of the Edgar, Agatha, Anthony, and Macavity awards, MWA Grand Master **MARGARET MARON** is on the reading lists of various courses in contemporary Southern literature. She served as president of Sisters in Crime and Mystery Writers of America. In 2008, she received the North Carolina Award, the state's highest civilian honor. Her latest book is *Designated Daughters*.

BEN H. WINTERS

Detective Palace's Three-Egg Omelet

Hank Palace, the hero of my novel *The Last Policeman,* is a young detective trying to solve a murder in a society in bad decline. With the apocalypse less than a year away, it's getting mighty tricky to get a good restaurant meal. Hank's whole modus operandi is to keep his head down and do his job, regardless of what's going on out in the panicky world; it's lucky for him that the folks at his favorite local diner feel the same way. He has been eating at the Somerset since he was in high school, and all that time he's been served by the same waitress, Ruth-Ann. Ruth-Ann teases Hank because he always gets the same darn thing, the three-egg omelet. But hey, an omelet is delicious and quick to eat, so you've got time left over to sip coffee and develop theories of the investigation.

That's just how Hank Palace is: he likes his routine; he likes things to persist in the way they always have been. Sure, the world is about to end—but I'd like the three-egg omelet, please.

Serve with whole wheat toast (heavily buttered) and coffee (black and hot). Ruth-Ann usually serves a little bowl of fruit with it, but Palace never eats it.

YIELD: 1 OMELET

3 eggs
A couple pats of butter
3 tablespoons milk
Salt and pepper
A sprig of parsley

1. Beat the eggs in a bowl. Heat a nonstick pan over medium heat. (Unless you've got a diner-style griddle, or one of those things you put over your stovetop to make it into a diner-style griddle.)

2. Get the butter melting in the pan. Pour the milk into the eggs, add salt and pepper to taste, and whisk. Whisk some more. Put your back into it.

3. When the pan is hot enough—i.e., when you flick some water in there and it hisses back at you—pour in the eggs. Leave them alone for about a minute, or a little less, until the bottom starts to set.

4. Use a spatula to push one edge of the omelet toward the middle of the pan, simultaneously tilting it to let the liquid part come in underneath it. Keep doing this until there's no more liquid. Flip it over (use two spatulas if you have to) and cook for another five seconds, until it looks cooked.

5. Now you could add fillings, like grated cheese or cooked mushrooms or, I don't know, green pepper or some such. Palace likes just the eggs.

6. Ease half the omelet off the pan and fold the other half on top of it. Garnish with the parsley.

BEN H. WINTERS wrote the Edgar-winning *The Last Policeman* and its sequels, *Countdown City* and *World of Trouble*; his other work includes *Sense and Sensibility and Sea Monsters* and the Edgar-nominated young adult mystery *The Secret Life of Ms. Finkleman*. He lives in Indianapolis and at benhwinters.com.

J. A. JANCE

Sugarloaf Café Sweet Rolls

In the first Ali Reynolds book, *Edge of Evil*, Ali's life in California has been blown to smithereens. She's lost her news anchor position as a result of being considered over the hill, and her husband has decamped for greener pastures. Hoping to regain her equilibrium, she returns to her hometown, Sedona, Arizona, where her parents run a local diner, the Sugarloaf Café. The café is named in honor of one of Sedona's famous red rock formations of the same name.

The Sugarloaf Café is fictional, but it's a place that serves stick-to-your-ribs down-home cooking. Ali's father, Bob, works as short order chef, while Edie, her mother, bakes the restaurant's daily supply of goods.

One of the things I'm able to do, writing fiction, is to mix in things and people I like along with things and people I don't like. People who annoy me tend to show up in my books as bad guys, suspects, and, every once in a while, dead. As for things I do like? Cinnamon rolls have always been high on my list, and that's why the Sugarloaf sweet rolls came into my books. I like them.

Please remember, however, that I write *fiction*. For a long time, the Sugarloaf sweet rolls existed only in my books and my imagination. Although I smelled them baking only in my head, fans soon started smelling them in their heads, too, and they began writing to ask for the recipe.

For a while I was stumped. How could I send a recipe if the sweet rolls didn't actually exist? That's when my son, Tom Schilb, came to my rescue. He created the recipe for the Sugarloaf Café sweet rolls in real life, and now there's a restaurant in Tucson that makes and serves them every week.

YIELD: 8 LARGE ROLLS

DOUGH

4¾ cups plus ⅔ cup all-purpose flour, divided

Pinch freshly grated nutmeg

½ cup granulated sugar

1 teaspoon kosher salt

1 packet instant yeast

1 large egg plus 1 large egg yolk

1 cup warm water

½ cup sour cream (full fat)

1. In a large mixing bowl, sift together 4¾ cups of the flour and nutmeg, and then add sugar, salt, and yeast. Stir in egg, egg yolk, and warm water and knead for about 5 to 8 minutes, or until dough just turns into a smooth, elastic ball. Knead in sour cream and the remaining ⅔ cup flour just until the dough takes up the additional ingredients. The dough should be slightly wet and a little sticky.

2. Place in a lightly buttered bowl, cover, and set in a warm spot until dough has doubled in bulk, about an hour, depending on the temperature of your kitchen.

3. While dough is rising, use a spatula to combine brown sugar, nutmeg, cinnamon, corn syrup, and butter until uniform. Fold in pecans.

4. When dough has doubled in bulk, punch it down and transfer it to a lightly floured surface. Roll out dough to a rectangle approximately 17 inches wide, 14 inches long, and ⅛ inch thick. Sprinkle the filling

FILLING

1½ cups dark brown sugar

Pinch freshly grated nutmeg

⅛ teaspoon ground cinnamon

1 tablespoon corn syrup

3 tablespoons softened unsalted butter

6 ounces chopped pecans

1 large egg white

ICING

8 ounces cream cheese, room temperature

½ cup granulated sugar

Optional: orange zest to taste

⅓ cup heavy cream

over dough in an even layer, leaving approximately 1 inch at the top without filling; brush the unfilled edge with egg white.

5. Roll up dough to form a 17-inch log and let rest, seam side down, for a few minutes to form a good seal. With a knife, gently trim the uneven ends of the log, about ½ inch from each end; discard ends and then cut the log into 8 equal slices of approximately 2 inches.

6. Lightly coat two 8-by-8-by-2-inch cake pans with softened butter and dust with flour. Place rolls flat side down in the pans (4 rolls per pan), leaving equal space between rolls and the side of the pan.

7. Cover loosely with either parchment paper or plastic wrap and let rolls rise until they begin to touch and almost double in width. (You can also place the covered rolls in the refrigerator and let sit overnight. Bring them to room temperature before baking.)

8. Preheat oven to 325°F. Bake for 35 to 40 minutes, until just golden on top. While rolls are baking, prepare the icing by whisking together cream cheese and sugar (and optional orange zest). Add cream and mix until fully incorporated. Spread over the rolls immediately after removing them from the oven.

J. A. JANCE is the *New York Times* best-selling author of more than fifty mysteries in four different series featuring J. P. Beaumont, Joanna Brady, Ali Reynolds, and the Walker family. She is also the author of a moving volume of poetry, *After the Fire*. Her most recent book is *Cold Betrayal*, featuring Ali Reynolds. Born in South Dakota and raised in Arizona, she, with her husband, splits her time between Tucson, Arizona, and Bellevue, Washington.

MAX ALLAN COLLINS & BARBARA COLLINS

Holiday Eggs

Dearest ones! This is Vivian Borne speaking—that is, writing—from the Trash 'n' Treasures "Antiques" series, where a mouth-watering recipe is included in every book. I discovered this one in my psychiatrist's waiting room—this is not to be misconstrued as an admission of guilt! I am not necessarily the patient who tore out the magazine page, although whoever that person might be, I hope next time she will tear out the picture of the finished dish as well and not risk a delicious recipeless image causing further mental frustration among my doctor's other, far needier clients.

This recipe is absolutely foolproof—I've had good results both on and off my meds—and is ideal for any holiday breakfast. (One word of warning: several helpings may cause a guest to drop off to sleep during a dramatic holiday reading by their hostess.) But you needn't wait for a holiday! Sometimes when my darling daughter Brandy (divorced, living with me) is down in the doldrums and even her Prozac can't help, I whip up a batch. So enjoy!

YIELD: 6–8 SERVINGS

8 to 10 slices white bread

1 pound sausage

6 to 8 eggs

½ cup grated sharp cheddar cheese

½ cup grated Swiss cheese

½ cup canned mushrooms, drained (optional)

¾ cup half-and-half

1¼ cups milk

1 teaspoon Worcestershire sauce

1 teaspoon mustard

Salt and pepper to taste

1. Preheat oven to 350°F. Butter a 9-by-13-inch pan.

2. Cut crusts off the bread, cut the slices into cubes, and spread the pieces in the bottom of the pan.

3. Brown the sausage; crumble over bread cubes.

4. In a bowl, beat the eggs lightly. Add the cheeses, mushrooms (if using), half-and-half, milk, Worcestershire sauce, mustard, salt, and pepper. Pour into the baking pan.

5. Bake for 35 to 40 minutes.

MAX ALLAN COLLINS is the author of the Shamus-winning Nathan Heller historical thrillers (including *Ask Not*) and the graphic novel *Road to Perdition*, the basis for the Academy Award–winning film. His innovative 1970s Quarry series has been revived by Hard Case Crime (the latest is *Quarry's Choice*), and he has completed eight posthumous Mickey Spillane novels, including *King of the Weeds*.

BARBARA COLLINS is the coauthor of the award-winning Trash 'n' Treasures comic cozy mystery series, beginning with *Antiques Roadkill* and continuing through the current *Antiques Con*. The fourth book in the series, *Antiques Flee Market*, won the *Romantic Times* award for Best Humorous Mystery of 2008. She and Max have also written two stand-alone thrillers (*Bombshell* and *Regeneration*).

RICHARD CASTLE

Morning-After Hotcakes

A lot of people ask me when and how I knew I was in love with Detective Kate Beckett. I knew I was a goner when I woke up one morning with an irresistible urge to make her my signature pancakes.

We were investigating a killer who had confused Beckett with Nikki Heat, the fictional character she inspired. It had progressed to a point where I feared for Beckett's life and wanted to protect her (though, admittedly, she is the one with the gun). I figured, spending the night on her couch, I could at the very least be an early warning system. As it turned out, the only disturbance that night was the raging sexual tension between her couch and the bedroom door. So when I woke up the first thing I thought of were . . . pancakes. The only times I've ever wanted to make pancakes have been when I wanted to cheer up someone I love. Simple as that, pancakes equal love. So does a good cup of coffee, but pancakes, those are serious.

YIELD: ABOUT 8 PANCAKES

2 cups all-purpose flour

¼ cup granulated sugar

2¼ teaspoons baking powder

½ teaspoon baking soda

½ teaspoon salt

2 eggs

2 cups buttermilk (or coconut milk or almond milk)

¼ cup melted unsalted butter, plus some for frying

Fresh fruit (sliced bananas, blueberries, chocolate chips . . . What? Chocolate chips are fruit!)

Maple syrup and whipped cream for serving

1. In a large bowl, sift together the flour, sugar, baking powder, baking soda, and salt.

2. Beat the eggs with the buttermilk and melted butter. Combine the dry and wet ingredients into a lumpy batter. Don't overmix!

3. Heat some butter in a skillet over medium heat. Spoon ⅓ cup batter into the skillet. Cook for 2 to 3 minutes on each side and then add fruit in the shape of the emoticon or smiley face of your choice. (The fruit can also be mixed into the batter before cooking if your philosophy is "more is more.")

4. Top with maple syrup and whipped cream and eat with someone you love.

Recipe from special guest Richard Castle of ABC's hit show Castle

RICHARD CASTLE is the author of numerous best sellers, including *Heat Wave*, *Naked Heat*, *Heat Rises*, and the Derrick Storm e-book original trilogy. His latest is the sixth Nikki Heat book, *Raging Heat*. He consults with the NYPD's 12th Precinct on New York's strangest homicides. Mr. Castle lives in Manhattan with his daughter and mother, both of whom infuse his life with humor and inspiration.

TAMMY KAEHLER

Simple, Speedy Gluten-Free Banana Bread

I've always got bananas in the house, and inevitably, they ripen. Since I won't eat bananas with brown spots (ick), I whip up some banana bread instead. However anyone who knows me is laughing by now, because I'm no cook. So this recipe is simple.

The other catch? I've got celiac disease, which means I'm allergic to gluten. So I modified a regular recipe. I went with an all-purpose gluten-free flour mix, as well as my favorite flour: teff, a grain from Ethiopia with a rich, dark flavor and lots of calcium, iron, protein, and fiber. As I perfected the recipe week after week, I also swapped brown sugar for white and tossed in whatever else I felt like that week—vanilla, cinnamon, walnuts, pecans, or chocolate chips (most often the chocolate, let's be honest).

The result? A snack that's bready and a little sweet—but not too sweet—and good any time of day or night. Looking back, I'm convinced my second racing mystery was powered by my teff banana bread.

Note: I've mixed these ingredients without the proper preparation or in the wrong order, and the bread always turned out great.

YIELD: 8–12 SERVINGS

1 cup all-purpose flour (gluten free or regular)

1 cup teff flour

1 teaspoon baking soda

¼ teaspoon salt

1 teaspoon ground cinnamon (optional)

½ cup butter, softened

¾ cup brown sugar

2⅓ cups mashed overripe bananas (the more, the moister and banana-y-er the bread turns out)

2 eggs, beaten

2 teaspoons vanilla extract (optional)

¼ to ½ cup or more nuts or chocolate chips (optional)

1. Preheat oven to 350°F. Lightly grease a 9-by-5-inch loaf pan (or line it with parchment paper).

2. In a large bowl, combine flours, baking soda, and salt. Add cinnamon, if using. Mix together lightly.

3. Cream together butter and brown sugar.

4. In a separate bowl, mash the bananas and stir in the eggs. Combine the banana-egg mixture with the butter-sugar mixture. Add vanilla if using. Mix thoroughly.

5. Stir the wet mixture into the dry mixture. Add nuts or chocolate chips, if using. Pour batter into the prepared pan.

6. Bake for 50 to 65 minutes, until a toothpick inserted into the center comes out clean.

7. Immediately remove loaf from the pan (easy to do with parchment paper) and place on a wire rack to cool for at least 10 minutes before eating. I wait at least 20 minutes, because gluten-free flour doesn't always taste good hot.

TAMMY KAEHLER created the Kate Reilly Racing Mystery Series to share the dramatic, competitive, and friendly world of racing with readers. Mystery fans and racing insiders alike praised the first two books. She takes readers behind the wheel a third time in *Avoidable Contact*. Visit her at tammykaehler.com.

KAREN HARPER

Zucchini Bread

As I've visited Amish country to research my nine mysteries set among the Plain People, I've also "researched" their cooking in local restaurants. The Amish say their lives are "not all cakes and pies," and that's true—they also enjoy food fresh from their gardens. This recipe is one my family has used for years. Though it could easily have come from Amish country, I actually learned it from my mother.

YIELD: 2 LOAVES

1 cup vegetable oil

2 cups granulated sugar

3 eggs, beaten

3 cups all-purpose flour

¼ teaspoon baking powder

1 teaspoon baking soda

1 teaspoon salt

1 teaspoon ground
cinnamon

2 cups finely chopped or
grated raw zucchini
(I include some of the
zucchini skin; it makes
the bread attractive)

1 cup chopped nuts
(walnuts or pecans
are best)

2 teaspoons vanilla extract

1. Preheat oven to 350°F. Grease and flour two 9-by-5-by-3-inch glass or metal pans.

2. In a bowl combine ingredients in the order they are listed and mix with a spoon as you go.

3. Pour mixture into prepared pans and bake for 50 minutes, or until a knife inserted into the center comes out clean.

4. Place pans on a wire rack to cool until you can handle them. Then tap the loaves out and let them cool a bit more on the rack.

KAREN HARPER is a *New York Times* best-selling author of contemporary suspense and historical fiction. *Dark Angel* won the Mary Higgins Clark Award. Her most recent release is the Cold Creek Trilogy, set in Appalachia: *Shattered Secrets*, *Forbidden Ground*, and *Broken Bonds*. Visit her website: karenharperauthor.com.

FRANKIE Y. BAILEY

Whole Wheat Wild Blueberry Lemon Pecan Muffins

This recipe was inspired by a scene in *The Red Queen Dies*, the first book in my near-future police procedural series. My protagonist, Albany police detective Hannah McCabe, stops at her favorite bakery on her way to work. She stands by the counter "munching on a lemon-blueberry-pecan muffin. Half a day's supply of antioxidants, and it even tasted like it was made with real sugar."

When I needed a recipe for the muffin in my book, I turned to my friend Dr. Alice Green, executive director of the Center for Law and Justice in Albany, New York. Alice is a superb cook. She tried several versions, using her family as taste testers. When I tried to make her muffins, I forgot to thaw the blueberries. I also used regular blueberries because I couldn't find wild blueberries. Even so, they came out well.

Bake these a few hours before serving them. The lemon flavor gets more intense as the muffins cool.

YIELD: 12 MUFFINS

MUFFINS
1 egg

1 cup skim milk

2 teaspoons lemon juice

½ cup plain nonfat Greek yogurt

1 cup all-purpose flour

1 cup whole wheat flour

¼ cup granulated sugar

2 teaspoons baking powder

1 teaspoon salt

½ cup chopped pecans

½ cup frozen wild blueberries, thawed, or 1 cup fresh wild blueberries

ICING
2 cups powdered sugar

1 tablespoon softened butter

Juice of 2 lemons

1. Preheat oven to 400°F. Grease the bottoms of 12 medium muffin cups.

2. Beat egg with milk and lemon juice. Add yogurt and beat until well mixed.

3. Mix in next 5 ingredients. Fold in pecans and blueberries. The batter should be lumpy.

4. Fill muffin cups with batter until two-thirds full. Bake for 20 minutes or until golden brown. Remove from pan and let cool completely.

5. Make the icing: Gradually add powdered sugar to butter, mixing to combine. Add lemon juice, a little at a time, and stir until creamy. Frost each cooled muffin with lemon icing.

FRANKIE Y. BAILEY is a criminologist whose mystery series feature police detective Hannah McCabe and crime historian Lizzie Stuart. Her recent publications are "In Her Fashion" (EQMM, 2014) and *What the Fly Saw* (Minotaur, 2015). Frankie is a past executive vice president of Mystery Writers of America and past president of Sisters in Crime.

CHAPTER TWO

The victim was alone. The door was locked
from the inside. No one could possibly have
entered or left, and all the suspects have
alibis. So ~~who~~ who brought in the appetizers?

ADRIENNE BARBEAU

Aunty Ruby's Yalanchi

(aka the Best Stuffed Grape Leaves You've Ever Had)

*"Peter ordered meza—a large plate of appetizers SuzieQ could share with us
(and no one would notice if I didn't eat)—yalanchi, souboereg, tourshou,
keufteh, little squares of lahmajoon, and taramasalata, hummus, and tabouli
for scooping onto pita. I felt like I was back in the old country again."*

Even though she's Armenian, Ovsanna Moore doesn't eat the appetizers she describes in this scene from *Love Bites*.

She's a vampyre, after all.

But she doesn't know what she's missing. This recipe came to me from one of my Armenian heroines, my 98-year-old aunt, Ruby Barton, to whom I dedicated *Vampyres of Hollywood*. Aunty Ruby hasn't had time to read the book, though. She's too busy rolling grape leaves. Her yalanchi gets eaten faster than any of Ovsanna's dinner dates.

Yours will, too.

**YIELD: ABOUT
80 PIECES**

2½ pounds onions (5 or 6), chopped

1 cup olive oil, plus more for serving

⅓ cup lemon juice, plus more for serving

½ bunch parsley, chopped

A few sprigs dill

2 cups long grain rice

4 cups boiling water, plus more for cooking

Salt and pepper

1 1-quart jar tender grape vine leaves

1. Sauté onions in olive oil in a large pan until translucent and on their way to golden brown. Add lemon juice, parsley, dill, rice, and boiling water. Season with salt and pepper to taste. Bring to a boil and then simmer on low heat, covered, for 30 minutes or until rice is cooked. Let cool.

2. Rinse grape leaves. Open one leaf at a time, placing flat on a plate or prep surface. Place 1 teaspoon rice mixture at top end of each leaf, centering it over the stem, and roll down the top of the leaf. Fold each side of the leaf into the middle and continue rolling down to the end.

3. Place the yalanchi in layers in a large pot. Cover the top layer with additional vine leaves. Add enough boiling water to almost reach the bottom of the top layer.

4. Cover pot and simmer on very low heat for an additional 40 minutes.

5. Serve yalanchi cold, drizzled lightly with olive oil and lemon juice.

ADRIENNE BARBEAU is an award-winning actress, a best-selling author, and the mother of three magnificent young men. *There Are Worse Things I Could Do* is her memoir. *Vampyres of Hollywood* and *Love Bites* are the first two novels in her comedy vampire detective series. *Make Me Dead* is on its way.

QUEEN OF CRIME
AND HIGH PRIESTESS OF POISON

GUNS, KNIVES, AXES, NOOSES, TRUNCHEONS. AGATHA CHRISTIE employed them all in her mysteries. But the murder weapon of choice for the best-selling novelist and crime writer of all time was poison. In over half of her sixty-six novels (which have sold roughly four billion copies), one or more victims is poisoned.

According to Michael C. Gerald, author of *The Poisonous Pen of Agatha Christie*, it was Christie's work as a hospital pharmacy dispenser during both world wars that gave her an appreciation of drugs as therapeutic agents as well as poison, and she relied on that knowledge to cleverly weave these substances into her plots. Dame Christie, who, by the way, was the first recipient of the Grand Master award from Mystery Writers of America, killed off characters with a variety of poisons, including arsenic, belladonna, strychnine, anthrax, digitoxin, nicotine, hemlock, snake venom, and, her favorite (featured in six books), cyanide.

Here are some of the foods and drinks that are doctored with poison in her books:

COFFEE | TEA | HOT COCOA | GIN | BEER | WHISKEY
CHAMPAGNE | WINE | PORT | MILK | WATER | TRIFLE
CHOCOLATES | FIG PASTE | MARMALADE | CURRY

—**Kate White**

NELSON DeMILLE

Male Chauvinist Pigs in the Blanket

This recipe is the favorite of my series character John Corey, a former NYPD homicide detective now working for the Federal Anti-Terrorist Task Force. Corey got this secret recipe by pocketing a few pigs from a Second Avenue pub and reverse-engineering the morsels in his kitchen.

As best Corey can figure, you start with hot dogs—as many as you can eat while watching a sporting event on TV. You should use butcher's dogs, which are firm and use real intestines for the casing. But you can also use supermarket dogs—Nathan's, Ball Park, Sabrett, whatever is around.

YIELD: 8 SERVINGS

8 hot dogs

1 can beer

Chili powder, to taste

1 8-ounce package Pillsbury crescent dinner rolls

French's yellow mustard in a squeeze bottle

1. Cut the dogs at right angles with a sharp instrument, though you can also use a blunt force object like the edge of a spatula to whack the dogs into bite-size pieces. Do this on a hard surface.

2. Next, put the dogs in a bowl or something and pour a can of beer over them. Let sit until the foam goes down, then drain the beer into a glass and drink it.

3. Sprinkle the dogs with chili powder. This is the secret ingredient that Corey figured out from dissecting the purloined pigs.

4. Now take the Pillsbury dough and do what it says on the package to make pigs in a blanket. The secret here is to add 5 minutes of baking time to what it says because of the beer. Or 10 minutes if you're in, like, Denver way above sea level. Keep checking with a flashlight until the crust is one shade lighter than the dog. Be patient.

5. Take the pigs out of the oven or toaster oven. Never use a microwave. It does something weird to the beer.

6. Put the pigs in the same bowl you used to soak the dogs in the beer. If serving to guests, everyone should have their own squeeze bottle of French's yellow mustard. *Never* use the thick, grainy mustard. It doesn't stick to the pigs.

7. The pigs will be hot for a while, but you can cool them by tossing them from hand to hand before squeezing the mustard on them. Chase with cold beer. Enjoy the game.

NELSON DeMILLE is the *New York Times* best-selling author of 18 books, including his John Corey series: *Plum Island*, *The Lion's Game*, *Night Fall*, *Wild Fire*, *The Lion*, and *The Panther*. He is working on a new John Corey novel, *A Quiet End*, to be published in Spring 2015.

KATE WHITE

A Very Sneaky Bean Dip

I wrote my first eight mysteries and suspense novels during the fourteen years I was editor-in-chief of *Cosmopolitan* magazine, which was a ridiculously insane thing to do, but I felt that if I didn't finally take a stab, so to speak, at being a mystery author, I would miss the chance entirely. After dropping my kids off at school each day, I went to the office and wrote for an hour before my staff arrived. In some ways, having a set but limited amount of time was a blessing; it made it easier not to procrastinate.

Because of how nutty my life was at that time (I once arrived at the office wearing two different shoes!), I was always looking for great time-management tricks and shortcuts that would make things a bit simpler. I was also constantly on the hunt for easy-peasy recipes to prepare, since I enjoyed cooking for my family and friends.

This is a recipe I learned from my mom, a fabulous woman who also writes mysteries (*Secrets Dark and Deep* and *Best Laid Plans*, to name two), and I've made it countless times for my husband and children as well as for company. Versions of this dish have appeared over the years, but I love this one because it's super simple and really tasty. Even sophisticated foodies have asked me for a copy of it.

YIELD: 6–8 SERVINGS

1 16-ounce can refried beans

1 15½-ounce jar salsa (whatever intensity you prefer)

1 cup grated cheddar cheese

1 cup grated Monterey Jack cheese

Taco chips or pita bread, for serving

1. Preheat oven to 350°F.

2. Spray an 8-inch baking dish with a little cooking spray.

3. Spread beans over the bottom of the dish.

4. Spread salsa over the beans.

5. Sprinkle both cheeses over the top.

6. Bake for 20 to 30 minutes, until cheese is bubbly hot and just starting to brown.

7. Present with a basket of taco chips or pita bread.

KATE WHITE, the former editor-in-chief of *Cosmopolitan* magazine, is the *New York Times* best-selling author of six Bailey Weggins mysteries as well as four stand-alone novels of suspense, including *The Wrong Man* (2015). She is also the editor of this cookbook.

HARLAN COBEN

Myron's Crabmeat Dip

Myron Bolitar, the sports agent protagonist of my series, is not much of a gourmet. His contribution to the culinary arts is usually limited to making observations like "a burger so rare it screamed ouch." This is probably due to the fact that his mother never cooked. But not long ago, Myron found this old recipe in the kitchen of his sidekick, Win. For those who know Win's taste in women, we can assume that one of Win's old girlfriends used to make it for him.

YIELD: 18 SERVINGS

3 large (8-ounce) packages cream cheese

3 large (6-ounce) cans crabmeat

½ cup Miracle Whip

2 teaspoons French mustard

⅔ cup dry white wine

2 teaspoons powdered sugar

1 teaspoon onion powder

Dash Lawry's seasoned salt

Dash garlic salt

Mix ingredients together while heating on stove. Serve warm.

Note: This dip freezes well.

With over 60 million books in print worldwide, **HARLAN COBEN** had his last seven consecutive novels *Missing You, Six Years, Stay Close, Live Wire, Caught, Long Lost,* and *Hold Tight* all debut at #1 on the *New York Times* Best-Seller List and on lists around the world.

CATHERINE COULTER

Big Bang Guacamole

Prepare to become an expert on the most outstanding guacamole in the known universe. Indeed, this recipe is even footnoted in *The Hitchhiker's Guide to the Galaxy* (well, it should have been). In my FBI series, Special Agents crowd into the Savich and Sherlock living room on football Sundays to chow down S&S's superb guacamole. (I start salivating when writing these scenes.) I personally can't pass an entire four quarters of football without stuffing my face. So follow my easy, perfect instructions and make your reputation. Don't forget, avocados are one of the top fifteen perfect foods, so this wonderful green creation is blessed by nutritionists everywhere.

YIELD: 4 SERVINGS

2 to 3 very ripe avocados

Enough lemon juice to soak the avocados

2 Roma tomatoes

Lots of scallions (or red onion if you prefer)

Salt, black pepper, and garlic salt, to taste

1 tablespoon nonfat sour cream

3 drops Tabasco sauce

Dollop Miracle Whip Light

Tortilla chips for serving (I like Primavera brand)

1. Mash avocados. Immediately add lots of lemon juice.

2. Cut up tomatoes and wring out all juice; add to avocado.

3. Cut scallions into small pieces; add to avocado.

4. Add salt, pepper, garlic salt, sour cream, and Tabasco, taste, and add more of whatever you deem necessary. Always have both a man and a woman taste—and then you decide.

5. Add a dollop of Miracle Whip Lite, not too much, just enough to make the mixture smooth and lighten the color a bit.

6. Heat tortilla chips in a 400°F oven just to warm them, up to 5 minutes (but watch them carefully so they don't burn). Remove from oven and sprinkle with salt.

7. Turn on football and serve.

8. Wallow in bliss. Eating guacamole and chips while reading one of my books would be even better.

New York Times best-selling author **CATHERINE COULTER** has written seventy-two books. *Power Play* is the eighteenth book in her wildly popular FBI thriller series. Coulter has also raised the bar with her new action-packed suspense series A Brit in the FBI. Her latest is *The Lost Key*.

SANDRA BROWN
Mystery Crackers

When I began writing over thirty years ago, I sought the advice of an indie bookstore owner in Lufkin, Texas, population 30,000. Mary Lynn Baxter was well known to every editor in New York because she did such a phenomenal trade in a relatively small market. She received advance reading copies from dozens of editors who valued her input, particularly her opinion of new writers.

As yet unpublished, I met Mary Lynn at a writers' conference in Houston. During our chat, she graciously offered to read a finished manuscript. In—what became familiar to me—her characteristic candor, she said, "I'll tell you whether or not it's any good."

I sent a manuscript to her. She liked it, called an editor at Bantam, and urged the woman to look for my submission in her slush pile. The editor bought that manuscript—and four others.

To this day, I owe my friend Mary Lynn a debt of gratitude I can never repay.

I also owe her for this recipe.

My rule for making any recipe is that it has no more than five ingredients. Counting the crackers, this has only four. It's easy for me to volunteer to take an appetizer to a dinner party. I can make Mystery Crackers while I'm writing. And I keep them in the fridge of my office for snacking. If I'm in a lull, I can nibble a few to "spice things up!"

YIELD: ABOUT 40 SERVINGS

1⅓ cups vegetable oil

1 packet dry ranch dressing mix

1 to 2 tablespoons cayenne or ground red pepper (depending on how spicy you want them)

1 1-pound box Premium saltines (all four sleeves)

1. Combine oil, dressing mix, and pepper.

2. Empty crackers into a 2-gallon ziplock bag and pour oil mixture over them. Seal and toss to coat crackers.

3. Over the next 6 to 8 hours, toss periodically until all the oil is absorbed into the crackers. Despite the oil, they'll retain their crunch and won't get soggy. I *swear*. I don't know how it works. It's a mystery!

Past MWA president **SANDRA BROWN** has written over sixty *New York Times* best sellers, and eighty million copies of her books are in print worldwide. Three books were made into TV movies, and she's been featured on two shows that document true crimes. Her new novel is *Mean Streak*.

LAURA LIPPMAN

Aunt Effie's Salmon Ball

My Aunt Effie—actually my great aunt—was a Capital-C Character, an old-fashioned steel magnolia with a hearty laugh and the first person who ever assured me I was funny. Also, maybe the last. Aunt Effie was the middle of three girls, brought up in an all-female household in Smalltown, Georgia, my great-grandmother having been widowed at a relatively young age. Aunt Effie herself was widowed twice and she learned to take care of herself, ending up in another all-female household with her daughter and granddaughter. Well, there was a poodle name John, but they painted his toenails, poor thing.

On top of everything else, she was a terrific hostess, and two of my favorite recipes come from her: cheese straws and a so-called Salmon Ball, although I despaired years ago of ever learning how to roll this concoction in slivered almonds, so I just mix it up and put it in a small dish. In fact, it makes a great hostess gift. It's really simple and everyone loves it. Not quite a health food, but you can substitute low-fat cream cheese for the hardcore stuff.

Because my household is peripatetic, I often find myself in a different city than the one where I keep all my family recipes. But my Aunt Effie's salmon ball is very forgiving, which is one reason I like to make it.

YIELD: 8–10 SERVINGS

1 teaspoon dried minced onions (available in the spice aisle)

1 tablespoon lemon juice

1 large can salmon, around 15 ounces

8 ounces cream cheese

1 teaspoon Worcestershire sauce

1 teaspoon prepared horseradish

1 teaspoon liquid smoke— if you can find it

Slivered almonds (optional)

Chopped parsley (optional)

1. Soak dried minced onions in lemon juice for 5 minutes.

2. Meanwhile, drain salmon and mix thoroughly with cream cheese.

3. Add lemon juice and onions to salmon mixture, along with Worcestershire, horseradish, and liquid smoke. You can add more or less according to your taste.

4. If you are nimble and wildly ambitious, you can form the mixture into a ball and roll it in slivered almonds and parsley. Frankly, I started omitting that step years ago because I could never get it to look right, although I suspect it might work better if you slightly chill the salmon mixture first. Me, I just put it in a nice piece of crockery and refrigerate for several hours. Serve with crackers; it also pairs well with a dry martini or the cocktail of your choice. Eat the leftovers on bagels.

LAURA LIPPMAN is an award-winning crime writer who has written nineteen books, the most recent of which is the *New York Times* best seller *After I'm Gone*. She lives in Baltimore and New Orleans.

SUSAN M. BOYER
Mamma's Pimento Cheese

Pimento cheese is a Southern staple from way back. When I was a child, we made sandwiches with it, and if we were getting fancy, we might grill the sandwich in a pan with butter. My mouth waters like one of Pavlov's dogs at the thought of a grilled pimento cheese sandwich with tomato soup. Occasionally, my mother would stuff celery sticks with pimento cheese. Nowadays, restaurants specializing in nouveau Southern cuisine are using pimento cheese as an ingredient in everything from fried green tomato napoleons to a topping for French fries.

Liz Talbot, my Southern private eye, loves pimento cheese as much as I do. And while she's never tasted a variation she didn't like, she loves her mamma's best. In *Lowcountry Bombshell*, Carolyn Talbot makes a batch of pimento cheese, and per usual there's enough to share. Liz gets a bowl for herself, which she rations, because while it is tasty, Mamma's pimento cheese is no one's idea of health food.

I invented this recipe myself because my sister-in-law, who makes truly remarkable pimento cheese, cooks like I do—a little of this, a little of that. When she shared her recipe, it was verbally, over a glass of wine, at the family Christmas party. I couldn't remember it, of course. But I had fun making up my own. This recipe makes roughly three quarts—plenty to share. It takes about an hour to make, but you can enjoy the results for weeks. I hope you like it as much as Liz and I do!

YIELD: 3 QUARTS

4 4-ounce jars diced pimentos (or 1 16-ounce jar if the store you shop has it)

Roughly 2 pounds Wisconsin red hoop cheese

1 pound Vermont white cheddar cheese

1½ pounds white aged cheddar cheese (sharp and nutty)

½ pound extra-sharp yellow cheddar cheese

8 ounces cream cheese, softened

2½ cups mayonnaise (I prefer Duke's)

½ cup sour cream

1. Place the pimentos in a very fine strainer to drain.

2. Shred the four cheeses and mix together in a very large bowl. Set aside.

3. Using an electric mixer, beat the cream cheese in a separate bowl until fluffy.

4. One at a time, add the mayonnaise, sour cream, and onions with their liquid to the cream cheese, blending after each addition.

5. Add salt, black and red pepper, Worcestershire sauce, and garlic powder and blend thoroughly.

6. Pour mixture over the shredded cheeses and stir gently until all the cheese is moist and the spread has a uniform appearance.

7. Stir in drained pimentos and chives.

8. Cover and refrigerate, preferably for at least four hours. The consistency will firm considerably if the pimento cheese refrigerates overnight. It will keep in your refrigerator for weeks but never lasts that long in ours. I give it out in small disposable food storage containers to family and friends.

½ sweet onion, shredded till it's pulpy (keep the liquid)

1 teaspoon sea salt

¾ teaspoon black pepper

1 teaspoon red pepper

1 tablespoon plus 1 teaspoon Worcestershire sauce

1 teaspoon garlic powder

3 tablespoons chives

Use it as a spread on crackers, pita bread, celery—practically anything. And don't forget to grill yourself a sandwich and have it with tomato soup.

Note: Please don't buy preshredded cheeses. You really won't like the results as much—I promise. Other cheeses may be substituted for variation and according to taste.

SUSAN M. BOYER writes the Liz Talbot mystery series. Her debut novel, *Lowcountry Boil*, is a *USA Today* best seller and an Agatha Award winner for Best First Novel. *Lowcountry Bombshell* is the second title in the series. *Lowcountry Boneyard* is due out in 2015. Susan lives with her husband and an inordinate number of houseplants in Greenville, South Carolina. For more information, visit susanmboyerbooks.com.

KATHLEEN ANTRIM

Cheesy Garlic Artichoke Dip

Journalist Jack Rudly, from my novel *Capital Offense,* was born in Missouri. The son of a diplomat, Jack grew up all over the globe and learned to speak five languages. Even with exposure to the best cuisine the world has to offer, it was his mother's Midwestern cooking that held his heart—his all-time favorite being her Cheesy Artichoke Dip. Every year on his birthday, no matter where they were in the world, Jack always requested this appetizer. He hopes you'll enjoy it as much as he has.

YIELD: 6–8 SERVINGS

1 large round loaf sour-dough bread

2 tablespoons butter

1 bunch green onions, chopped

12 cloves garlic, minced

8 ounces cream cheese, room temperature, cut into small cubes

1 cup sour cream

1 cup shredded medium cheddar cheese

2 10-ounce cans water-packed artichoke hearts, drained and lightly chopped

2 sourdough baguettes, sliced into thin rounds

1. Preheat oven to 350°F.

2. Cut a hole in the top of the sourdough round and set aside; do not discard the piece you cut. Remove most of the soft inside loaf, leaving enough bread so it holds its shape; it will be the serving bowl for the dip.

3. Melt butter in a sauté pan. Add green onions and sauté for about 1 to 2 minutes. Add garlic and sauté for another 1 to 2 minutes, until onions are soft and garlic is fragrant.

4. In a large bowl, combine the cream cheese, sour cream, cheddar cheese, and sautéed onions and garlic. Mix well.

5. Fold in the artichokes.

6. Scoop the artichoke/cheese mixture into the hollowed-out sourdough round and place the top over the hole in the bread.

7. Wrap the loaf in a double layer of heavy-duty aluminum foil and bake for $1\frac{1}{2}$ to 2 hours.

8. Remove the loaf from the oven and remove the foil. Serve with the baguette slices.

KATHLEEN ANTRIM is the award-winning and best-selling author of *Capital Offense*. As a commentator, she wrote for the San Francisco and D.C. *Examiner* newspapers and was featured on HotTalk 560 radio and the syndicated *Battle Line*. Antrim is on the board of directors for the San Francisco Writers' Conference, past co-president of International Thriller Writers, and director of the ITW-USO.

KATHERINE HALL PAGE

Chèvre Endive Spears with Rubies

My protagonist, amateur sleuth Faith Fairchild, is a caterer, so food plays an important role in the series that started with *The Body in the Belfry*, twenty-three books ago. Readers tell me they get hungry as they read them. Faith is from the Big Apple with no intention of moving, but she falls in love with a New England minister who has just performed the service at a wedding she is catering. Soon she finds herself living in more bucolic orchards outside Boston and she starts up her firm, Have Faith, again, resolving to steer clear of too-typical New England fare like boiled dinners, bright red hot dogs, and Moxie. This appetizer is typical of the fare she creates—elegant, tasty, and simple—highlighting the ingredients in a nice presentation.

YIELD: 6 SERVINGS

2 heads endive (Look for endive that is fresh and has a tight head. If you can, find the slightly purple variety; it's nice to alternate the spears on your serving platter.)

Balsamic vinegar, to taste (Saporoso brand if possible)

5 ounces fresh chèvre, room temperature

4 ounces cream cheese, room temperature

1 tablespoon half-and-half or light cream

Pomegranate seeds

1. Discard the outer leaves of the endives and cut a thin slice from the bottom to make it easier to remove the spears. You may have to do this twice. Set aside the small core of inner leaves for a future salad.

2. Lightly brush the spears with vinegar. Arrange the spears attractively on a serving platter or tray.

3. Combine the cheeses and half-and-half in a food processor and pulse until creamed together. (Note: You can prepare the cheese mixture ahead of time and refrigerate, bringing it to room temperature before assembling.)

4. Fill a pastry bag with the mixture and pipe about 1 tablespoon onto the wide end of each spear. You may also spoon the mixture on the spear. Top with pomegranate seeds. Other topping choices are: walnut halves, pieces of fresh fig, or candied ginger. In season, sliced ripe strawberry is delicious.

KATHERINE HALL PAGE is the author of twenty-one Faith Fairchild mysteries, including five for younger readers, as well as a series cookbook *Have Faith in Your Kitchen*. She received Agathas for Best First Novel, Best Novel, and Best Short Story and was nominated for Edgar, Mary Higgins Clark, Macavity, and other awards. Her latest book is *Small Plates*, a collection of short fiction. Visit her online at katherine-hall-page.org.

CHAPTER THREE

We have two of the best grifters in the game. We also have a cat burglar, a lock pick, ~~and~~ a master forger, and homemade vegetable stock. If we can't make this soup work, no one can.

MODEL 1

LEA WAIT

Murderously Good Maine Chowdah

This was originally my grandmother's recipe, and it's still one of my favorite suppers. It can be made a day ahead and then heated after a day spent at an auction, an antiques show, or the beach. I often make it when guests are headed toward Maine (what we refer to as "Down East") but don't know precisely when they'll arrive! Gram Estelle Curtis, one of the protagonists in my Haven Harbor series, has this chowder ready when her granddaughter, Angie, arrives at home after a ten-year absence.

YIELD: VARIABLE

4 to 5 strips uncooked bacon, cut in small pieces

3 garlic cloves, diced

½ teaspoon salt, or to taste

1 teaspoon black pepper, or to taste

1 teaspoon cayenne pepper, or to taste

PER PERSON

½ yellow onion, diced

1 cup lobster broth (second choice, clam broth. Otherwise, chicken broth.)

2 medium potatoes cut in 1-inch pieces

½ pound white fish (preferably haddock), cut in ¾-inch pieces

½ pound shrimp or lobster meat, cut in ¾-inch pieces

½ cup light cream

2 tablespoons chopped fresh parsley

1. Heat bacon in a large pot. Add onion and garlic and stir over medium heat until you can see through the pieces of onion.

2. Pour in broth and add potatoes. (If the broth doesn't cover the potatoes, add a little water until they are covered.) Add salt, black pepper, and cayenne. Bring to a boil.

3. Reduce heat and simmer for about 10 minutes, or until you can easily stick a fork through a piece of potato.

4. Add fish and shellfish. Cook for another 5 to 10 minutes, until all is cooked. Then add light cream and heat until hot.

5. Stir in the parsley, and serve in bowls with oyster crackers or French bread.

Maine author **LEA WAIT** writes the Shadows Antique Mystery series, the Mainely Needlework series, and historical novels for ages 8 to 14 set in nineteenth-century Maine. Check her website, www.leawait.com, friend her on Facebook, and read the blog she writes with other mystery authors: mainecrimewriters.com.

CONNIE ARCHER

Chicken Artichoke Tarragon Soup

Shortly after the release of the first book in my "soup lover's mystery" series, I received a Facebook message from a reader who said she was devastated that the chef at the fictional By the Spoonful Soup Shop mentioned a chicken artichoke tarragon soup, but the recipe was not included at the end of the book. I went on a hunt through my recipes, finally found it, and tested it just to make sure everything was accurate. This soup turned out to be beyond my expectations and one of my favorites.

YIELD: 6 SERVINGS

2 tablespoons butter

1 shallot, chopped

2 heaping tablespoons dried tarragon (or fresh tarragon if available)

2 skinless boneless chicken breasts, cut into bite-size cubes

½ cup dry white wine

4 cups chicken broth or chicken stock

10 to 12 ounces water-packed artichoke hearts or quarters

½ cup uncooked pearl barley (rice can be substituted if preferred)

Fresh tarragon, for garnish

1. Melt the butter in a large pot. Add the shallot and tarragon and sauté for a few minutes.

2. Add the chicken to the pot and sauté for a few more minutes, just enough to allow it to pick up the flavor of the spices.

3. Pour in the wine and cook for another minute.

4. Add the chicken broth or stock, cover, and let simmer on low heat for approximately 15 minutes, just until the chicken pieces are thoroughly cooked. Scoop the chicken out of the pot and set aside.

5. Add the artichoke hearts and pearl barley, and cook on low to medium heat for another 15 minutes.

6. Turn off the heat, cover the pot, and let the ingredients sit for half an hour, until the barley has absorbed the liquid and expanded. Scoop out a little bit of barley and taste it to make sure it's softened.

7. Once the pot has cooled, puree the soup mixture.

8. Return the pureed soup and the chicken pieces to the pot, heat, and serve garnished with fresh tarragon.

CONNIE DI MARCO writes the national best-selling Soup Lover's Mystery series from Berkley Prime Crime under the name Connie Archer. *Ladle to the Grave* is the fourth in the series. You can visit her at conniearchermysteries.com to learn more about her mysteries and soup recipes.

J. T. ELLISON

Avgolemono

I'm late to soup making. For a decent cook, this is an embarrassing admission. But I've always been terrified of it, mostly because every time I've ever watched my mom make soup (turkey soup especially) there have been bones and carcasses involved. I prefer my carcasses inside the pages of my books, thank you very much.

I stumbled across a chicken soup recipe in a magazine a couple of years ago that called for chicken breasts, not the bones. Realizing I could use premade stock, I dove in. These two shortcuts have allowed me to finally master the (quite simple) art of soup making.

Avgolemono, Greek lemon chicken soup, was the second recipe I tried, gleaned from Pinterest, where it was posted by my friend Betsy Koch. I was sick with the flu and needed the comfort of chicken soup, and I had a slew of lemons left over from another dish. The perfect winter evening soup was born. I've taken the original recipe and modified it to my particular taste and weaknesses—extra lemony and no bones! A good mirepoix mix (the carrots, celery, and onion) is essential to this soup, so don't skimp.

This is a particularly lemony version of Avgolemono. If that makes you nervous, cut back the lemon whisked in with the eggs to $1/4$ cup and then add more to taste. Note: the lemon flavor gets more concentrated as the soup thickens. Use caution in using more than $1/2$ cup (the juice of 2 lemons).

Fresh parsley and/or dill are more than garnish with this soup. Don't skip them.

YIELD: 6–8 SERVINGS

2 tablespoons extra virgin olive oil (plus more if needed to brown chicken)

$1/2$ medium onion, diced small

2 stalks celery, diced small

2 large carrots, diced small

2 large chicken breasts, cut into 2-to-3-inch pieces of roughly equal thickness and seasoned generously with salt and pepper

2 quarts chicken stock

1 cup starchy rice, such as arborio, or orzo pasta (long grain brown rice works, too)

1. In a large pot, heat olive oil on medium heat. Sauté the onion, celery, and carrots until soft, about 5 minutes. Add the chicken pieces and about 1 tablespoon olive oil if needed. Brown chicken on both sides, stirring vegetables so they don't overbrown.

2. Add chicken stock, rice, and 1 teaspoon of the salt. Bring to a slow boil and then reduce heat to low. Simmer for about 30 minutes.

3. Transfer $1 1/2$ cups of the broth to a small bowl to cool slightly. Remove chicken with tongs and shred with a fork. Set aside.

4. In a medium bowl, whisk the eggs with the lemon juice. Whisk about $1/4$ cup of the reserved cooled chicken broth into the egg mixture to temper the eggs so they do not curdle. Repeat, slowly adding more broth as you whisk. After you've incorporated all the set-aside broth into the egg mixture, slowly add this mixture to the soup, whisking quickly to incorporate.

2 teaspoons salt,
 divided

3 eggs, whisked

½ cup fresh lemon juice
 (from 2 lemons)

1 to 2 teaspoons black
 pepper

Fresh parsley or dill,
 to taste

5. Return the shredded chicken to the pot and heat on low. Do not boil again. Add the black pepper and the remaining 1 teaspoon salt. Top with fresh parsley or dill, serve hot, and devour.

J. T. ELLISON is the *New York Times* best-selling author of multiple novels and short stories published in more than twenty countries. Her novel *The Cold Room* won the ITW Thriller Award for Best Paperback Original, and *Where All Dead Things Lie* was a RITA nominee for Best Romantic Suspense. She lives in Nashville with her husband. Her website is jtellison.com

THE FOOD HOUND OF BAKER STREET

AS ONE READS *THE ADVENTURES OF SHERLOCK HOLMES,* IT BECOMES CLEAR that the great detective loves to dine. His tastes run to sturdy British food at restaurants like Simpson's, where standing beef roasts, grouse, and lamb are elegantly served.*

Holmes's landlady, Mrs. Hudson, regularly provides him with hardy fare to eat. In "The Naval Treaty," Holmes points out that "her cuisine is limited but she has as good an idea of breakfast as a Scotchwoman." This means eggs, mushrooms, sausage, bacon, scones, and beans.

Food plays a role in several of Holmes's cases. In "The Dying Detective" he gives up eating for days to produce the drawn appearance necessary to set a trap for a miscreant.

And in "The Speckled Band," he sets out a saucer of milk to prove the presence in the house of a deadly, milk-drinking serpent.

No doubt Holmes knew of another use for milk common in prisons at the time: writing with it. Milk is invisible when it dries, but heating the words over a lamp makes the fat in the fluid brown so they may be read.

—E. J. WAGNER, crime historian and author of **The Science of Sherlock Holmes**

* Opened in 1828, Simpson's-on-the-Strand still exists in London. Charles Dickens and Vincent van Gogh reportedly dined there.

WENDY HORNSBY

Grand-Mère Marie's
Root Vegetable Vichyssoise

My family has always loved the French-style potato leek soup that is the base for the soup below. The original is more properly called *potage parisien* than vichyssoise because it is served hot, not cold, but eaten either way it is delicious.

During a winter trip to Normandy undertaken as research for *The Paramour's Daughter*, a Maggie MacGowen Mystery, we found that any dish that used fresh, locally grown vegetables meant a dish made with root vegetables and tubers. One very cold night, fresh vegetable soup turned out to be an approximation of the dish you find below. Thanks to a little instruction from the chef, I have been making Root Vegetable Vichyssoise ever since. In the book, when Maggie's French godmother cooks up a big pot of soup in a farm kitchen, this is the soup I knew she had to be making.

There is no way to make a small pot of soup, certainly not this one. Cook it on Sunday and eat it all week; it reheats beautifully. If you freeze a batch before step 5, you can have great soup all winter long.

YIELD: 8–10 SERVINGS

4 slices good, thick-cut bacon, such as smoked apple wood, snipped into 1-inch lengths, plus 2 whole slices reserved for garnish

2 tablespoons olive oil

1 pound leeks, halved lengthwise, carefully washed, and sliced into 1-inch half-rounds

3 to 4 garlic cloves, crushed or chopped

3 celery stalks, cut into 1-inch lengths, or 1 cup chopped celery root

1 to 2 pounds white potatoes, sliced into 1-inch-thick rounds

2 carrots, cut into 1-inch lengths, or 1 cup diced sweet potato or yam

1. Place the chopped bacon in a soup pot over medium heat and cook until transparent. Add the olive oil. Add the leeks, garlic, and celery (or celery root). Cover, and cook until the leeks sweat, 5 to 8 minutes.

2. Add all of the other vegetables, stock, and water. Give the pot a good stir, making sure the bacon is not stuck to the bottom. Bring to a boil. Immediately lower the heat, cover the pot, and simmer gently for about 2 hours, stirring occasionally. Do not let the pot come to a full boil again. If it does, add a little cold water or stock and lower the heat.

3. While the soup simmers, in a small sauté pan cook the 2 reserved slices of bacon until crisp. Cool, crumble, and set aside for garnish. Optionally, add 1 tablespoon or less of the bacon drippings to the soup.

4. Remove the pot from the heat. With an immersion blender, blend the contents of the pot until smooth. If using a standard blender or food processor, carefully transfer the hot mixture to the machine in batches, blending until smooth, and then transfer the blended soup to a second soup pot. If the soup is too thick, add additional water or stock. If it is too thin, uncover and let simmer gently until it reaches your preferred consistency. Move the pot away from the heat.

2 to 3 pounds any combination of the following, sliced or diced: 1 small turnip, 2 parsnips, 1 small rutabaga, 1 medium onion (you can use any root vegetable, but be sparing with strong-flavored roots and tubers such as daikon radish, red radish, beets, and fennel root)

2 quarts good chicken or vegetable stock, plus more as needed

1 quart water, plus more as needed

1 cup cream, buttermilk, or Greek yogurt

½ cup good, dry white wine (optional)

3 tablespoons butter

Salt and pepper (a dash of powdered chipotle or cayenne pepper never hurts)

1 teaspoon chopped fresh herb such as basil, parsley, or thyme, for garnish (optional)

5. Add the cream, white wine (if using), butter, and salt and pepper to taste. Add chipotle or cayenne pepper, if using. Ladle soup into bowls. Garnish each serving with a small dollop of cream, bacon crumbles, and (optional) a sprinkle of chopped fresh herb.

Note: All soup is better on the second day. You can make this soup ahead and store it for up to three days in the refrigerator, or freeze *before* adding the cream. To reheat, ladle enough for your meal into a saucepan, bring to serving temperature over low heat, and then add an appropriate proportion of cream, wine, and butter. Correct the seasonings, and serve as above. If you reheat the completed soup, use the lowest heat possible. Correct consistency if necessary by adding stock and a very small amount of cream.

WENDY HORNSBY is the Edgar Award–winning author of the Maggie MacGowen and Kate and Tejeda mysteries and many short stories. The early Maggie MacGowen books are again available via mysteriouspress.com and are available in most e-book formats. Her most recent book is *The Color of Light* (Perseverance Press, 2014).

DAVID HOUSEWRIGHT

Corn Chowder

One of the many advantages of being a crime novelist is that I get to work from home. Which means I also have plenty of time to cook—one of my favorite activities. Rushmore McKenzie, the protagonist of my current series of mysteries, also loves to cook and is forever hosting dinner parties so he can show off. The meals are always ones I've made myself, including this corn chowder recipe that I serve at my annual Christmas party. On the other hand, my other series hero—Holland Taylor—is barely able to use the microwave; go figure.

YIELD: 6–8 SERVINGS

3 cups water

4 cups diced potatoes

2 cups diced carrots

1 teaspoon salt

½ teaspoon black pepper

½ teaspoon dried thyme

¼ cup (½ stick) butter

¼ cup flour

2 cups milk

2 cans creamed corn

2 cups shredded cheddar cheese

1 pound bacon, fried and crumbled

1. Combine potatoes, carrots, and seasonings in a large pot; cook until vegetables are tender.

2. Melt butter over low heat in a separate saucepan. Add flour and cook until bubbly. Add milk, bring to a boil, and boil for 1 minute.

3. Add white sauce to vegetable mixture. Add creamed corn, cheese, and bacon. Heat until cheese is melted.

A reformed reporter and ad man, **DAVID HOUSEWRIGHT** won an Edgar Award and three Minnesota Book Awards. His seventeenth novel is *Unidentified Woman #15* (St. Martin's Minotaur). He was elected president of the Private Eye Writers of America in 2014.

WHAT EXACTLY IS A RED HERRING?

LITERALLY SPEAKING, A RED HERRING IS A FISH THAT HAS BEEN SMOKED until its flesh turns red. It is sometimes referred to as a kipper, and in the United Kingdom, it is often served for breakfast.

When it comes to mystery novels, a red herring is a false clue, one that's meant to mislead the reader about the true identity of the murderer. It might be an action taken by a character or simply a comment that is made.

A red herring is similar to the misdirection a magician uses to distract the audience so they don't see how a trick is accomplished. And just as magic wouldn't be any fun without misdirection, mysteries wouldn't be nearly as delicious without red herrings.

It was once thought that the nonliteral meaning of the term originated from the practice of using kippers to train hounds to follow a scent. But new research suggests there was no such practice. In 1807 the English polemicist William Cobbett apparently mentioned one occasion when he used a kipper to divert hounds from chasing a hare, and the words were later adopted to refer to a literary device.

False clues have been around from the beginning of crime fiction and were used by Arthur Conan Doyle and Edgar Allan Poe and, later, by Agatha Christie. For instance (spoiler alert), in her first novel, the *Mysterious Affair at Styles*, the two main characters appear to hate each other. Thus many readers are surprised when they eventually learn that the two colluded in the murder.

—**Kate White**

MARY HIGGINS CLARK

Mary's Celebratory Giants Game Night Chili

When the leaves begin to turn and there's a chill in the air, it means that the professional football season is about to begin. We go to most of the New York Giants' home games, but when the Giants are away, there isn't anything more fun for us than to have a pot of chili bubbling in a Crock-Pot while whoever is available in the family gathers to watch the game with my husband and me.

It's a Sunday afternoon or early evening ritual that we all love.

The bowls and silverware and napkins are on the sideboard. The wine glasses are on the bar ready to be filled. Warm Italian bread is next to the Crock-Pot. A fire flickering in the fireplace lends atmosphere, especially if the wind is whistling in the chimney. Halftime is dinnertime. The Giants are a champion team, but even if they lose, all is not doom and gloom. Chili is a great comfort food. I got the recipe from a caterer, Louis Del Vecchio, about thirty years ago and I haven't changed it one iota.

Just for the record, Louis cooks for us every night now. How lucky can you get!

YIELD: 8–10 SERVINGS

4 pounds ground beef

1 pound ground sausage

1 pound ground turkey

Salt, black pepper, and chili powder, to taste

1 large can crushed tomatoes

2 small cans diced tomatoes with jalapeño and onion

1 small onion, diced

1 bottle beer (your choice)

4 medium cans assorted red and black beans, rinsed thoroughly

Assorted spices to taste: cumin, garlic, cinnamon, crushed red pepper for additional "heat"

Seasoned bread crumbs (optional)

1. Preheat a large slow cooker according to the manufacturer's instructions.

2. Sauté all meats in batches so they brown rather than steam. Season each batch with salt, pepper, and chili powder to taste.

3. After browning the last batch of meat, drain most of the fat from the pan. Add onions and sauté. Deglaze the pan with a small amount of the beer.

4. Add all tomatoes, onions, meat, and beans to the slow cooker. Add one-fourth of the beer, 2 teaspoons chili powder, 1 teaspoon cumin, a very small pinch of cinnamon (not too much!), a shake or two of garlic powder, and black pepper to taste.

5. Let cook on high for 4 hours; stir well. Set the slow cooker to low; taste, and, if needed, add salt, pepper, chili powder, and/or a few crushed red pepper flakes.

6. After 2 hours on low, turn off the slow cooker or set to the warm setting until ready to serve. If there is too much liquid, stir in a scant amount of seasoned bread crumbs to thicken.

7. Serve chili with bowls of shredded cheddar cheese, sliced red onion, sour cream, and warm tortilla chips.

MARY HIGGINS CLARK's books are worldwide best sellers. In the United States alone, her books have sold over 100 million copies. Her latest suspense novel, *I've Got You under My Skin* (Simon & Schuster). She is the author of thirty-three previous suspense novels.

THOMAS H. COOK

Past as Prologue (Vegetarian) Chili

In many of my books, the past returns to haunt the present. So it does also with this recipe. When I wrote *Breakheart Hill*, many of my old friends from high school were delighted that I had mentioned a hometown favorite recipe known as Frito Pie. They were very pleased that this dish had imprinted itself upon my memory. Actually it hadn't. Instead, the dish that had truly captivated me was the chili served once a week at my public high school. After many efforts at duplicating this chili, I finally found the missing ingredient: peanut butter!

My original chili was made with ground beef, but because I have many vegetarian friends, and because I now try to include healthier choices in my diet, I use soy chorizo and find no loss in taste or texture.

The recipe below is very flexible in that each ingredient can be adjusted to taste. For people who want an extra layer of the exotic, a teaspoon of cumin, a half-cup of a hearty red wine in place of water, or a tablespoon of vinegar can also be added to the mix.

YIELD: 4 SERVINGS

2 tablespoons extra virgin olive oil

1 large onion, chopped

1 tablespoon chopped garlic

½ tablespoon red pepper flakes

1 12-ounce package soy chorizo (such as Trader Joe's)

2 tablespoons chili powder

1 28-ounce can crushed tomatoes

½ cup water (or red wine or stock)

1 tablespoon peanut butter

3 15½-ounce cans beans of your choice (red kidney, black, cannellini beans or a mix all work well)

1. In a 2-quart pot, heat the olive oil. Add the onion, garlic, and red pepper flakes and cook until onion is soft but not browned.

2. Crumble the chorizo into the mixture.

3. Add the chili powder, crushed tomatoes, and water, mix thoroughly, and continue to cook over medium heat.

4. Reduce the heat to low. Add the peanut butter and again mix thoroughly. Let simmer for 5 minutes, but avoid a rolling boil.

5. When the mixture is thoroughly cooked, add the beans and heat through. Or it may be frozen without the beans. Add the beans when you heat it to serve.

Note: When serving chili, I always have an array of garnishes, such as chopped raw onions or scallions, chopped jalapeños, diced tomatoes, a mix of diced of green, yellow, and red peppers, grated cheddar cheese (or the cheese of your choice), and sour cream. The chili can also be served over rice or, my favorite, crumbled Doritos.

THOMAS H. COOK is an internationally award-winning author. He has been nominated for Edgars eight times in five different categories, and his novel *The Chatham School Affair* won the Edgar for Best Novel in 1996. His latest novel is *A Dancer in the Dust*.

JOHN McEVOY

Gone Broke Goulash

Horse racing has long been a passion of mine, as reflected in my six mystery novels, the most recent of which is *High Stakes* (2014). Fact is, I have enjoyed watching thoroughbreds run, and betting on them, since I was a boy. They are marvelous animals to observe in action, ridden by arguably the best pound-for-pound athletes in the world. In the course of those more than several years, I have enjoyed some major wagering successes, one of which enabled me to purchase my first (preowned) car. But, of course, like the majority of my fellow enthusiasts, I have experienced far more losing days than ones blessed by bonanzas. As the old saw has it, "You can beat a race, but you can't beat the races."

I am still attempting to disprove that theory. I go along with the famous Calumet Farm groom nicknamed Slow 'n' Easy, who believed that a person should make a bet every day because "there's no telling when you might be walkin' around lucky." Of course, such a betting theory can also bring to mind another ancient maxim: "Chicken today, feathers tomorrow." This one has been attributed to a Louisville, Kentucky, newspaperman in 1896. I am sure such a truism has far earlier antecedents.

My afternoons at the racetrack that fell into the "feathers" category led directly to the necessary development of my recipe for Gone Broke Goulash.

This is an entrée that is attractively inexpensive, tasty, filling, not challenging to prepare even for culinary klutzes such as myself—and mighty damn handy when most of a person's bankroll is found to be sadly diminished. It is a dish not only very edible but eminently reheatable in case good fortune proves furtive on successive days, whether at the racetrack or in other commercial endeavors.

YIELD: NUMBER OF SERVINGS DETERMINED BY OUTCOME OF RECENT RACES
2 pounds ground beef
1 medium onion, finely chopped
1 green pepper, finely chopped
2 teaspoons garlic salt
1 8-ounce package flat noodles
1 8-ounce can tomato sauce
¼ cup ketchup

1. Brown the beef in skillet along with onion and pepper, adding garlic salt early on.

2. Boil noodles to a bit short of al dente. Add them to ground beef mixture.

3. Add tomato sauce and simmer mixture uncovered on low heat for 15 minutes. Then add ketchup and mix thoroughly.

Note: This dish is best served with peanut-buttered white bread accompanied by a chilled Dr. Pepper.

JOHN McEVOY, a former editor of *Daily Racing Form* and as always an active bettor, had his sixth horse racing mystery novel *High Stakes* published by Poisoned Pen Press. Two of his books have won Benjamin Franklin awards.

TWIST PHELAN

La Ristra's Carrot Soup with Thai Red Curry and Apple-Pear Chutney

La Ristra is a Pinnacle Peak tradition. The restaurant's signature dishes include the carrot soup with Thai red curry, made special by the addition of apple-pear chutney. My character Hannah Dain always orders this smooth but fiery delight when at La Ristra with her on-again, off-again boyfriend, Cooper Smith. And she isn't embarrassed to scrape the bottom of the bowl!

YIELD: 2–4 SERVINGS

CHUTNEY

2 firm-ripe red Bartlett pears

2 Granny Smith apples

1 cup golden raisins

½ cup unseasoned rice vinegar

¼ cup granulated sugar

1 tablespoon finely chopped fresh ginger

1 teaspoon mustard seeds

½ teaspoon cinnamon

SOUP

1 tablespoon canola oil

6 large carrots, sliced

2 ¼-inch slices ginger

1 medium white onion, finely chopped

4 cups vegetable stock

⅓ cup coconut milk

1 teaspoon red curry paste

Salt and pepper, to taste

1 scallion, cut into matchsticks

1 tablespoon cilantro

1. Make the chutney: Halve and core the pears and apples. Cut 2 pear halves and 2 apple halves into ¼-inch-thick slices, and chop the remaining pears and apples.

2. In a saucepan, combine the sliced and chopped pears and apples with the remaining chutney ingredients and bring to a simmer, stirring gently. Simmer, covered, stirring occasionally, until the fruit is just tender, 10 to 15 minutes, and then let cool. The chutney may be made one day ahead and chilled, covered. Let warm to room temperature before putting into soup bowls.

3. Make the soup: Heat the oil in a large saucepan. Add the carrots and ginger and cook over moderately high heat, stirring, until the carrots are crisp-tender and lightly browned, 6 to 7 minutes.

4. Add the onions and cook until soft but not browned, about 2 minutes.

5. Add the stock, 1½ cups water, coconut milk, and curry paste to the saucepan and bring to a boil. Simmer over moderate heat until the carrots are tender, about 25 minutes.

6. Using an immersion blender, puree the soup (or puree the soup in batches using a regular blender). Season with salt and pepper to taste.

7. To serve, spoon a heaping tablespoon of chutney into the bottom of each soup bowl. Ladle the soup on top, sprinkle with the scallion and cilantro, and serve.

TWIST PHELAN is the author of the critically acclaimed Pinnacle Peak mystery series (Poisoned Pen Press). Her short stories appear in Mystery Writers of America and "best of" anthologies and *Ellery Queen Mystery Magazine*, and have won or been nominated for the Thriller, Anthony, Ellis, and Derringer awards.

MARY ANN CORRIGAN

Take Your Pick Vegetable Salad

"Don't give me any turkey leftovers. All I want is some of your mother's vegetable salad." I hear similar requests after every holiday dinner. Just as I modified Mom's original 1970s recipe, the sleuth in my Five Ingredient Mysteries updates her grandmother's recipes from the same era, substituting fresh ingredients for canned. Take your pick—canned or fresh vegetables for this sweet-and-sour dish. Take your pick of vegetables, too. Add red peppers for seasonal color in December and carrots for a touch of autumn at Thanksgiving. The recipe's best feature: you marinate the vegetables for a day and have one less dish to prepare at the last minute.

YIELD: 10–12 SIDE DISH SERVINGS

2 cups uncooked zucchini sliced in ¼-inch rounds

1 pound cut green beans (if fresh, blanch for 2 minutes and plunge into ice water)

1 14-ounce can artichoke hearts, quartered

4 ounces fresh mushrooms, sliced ¼ inch thick

1 medium onion, sliced

1 cup pitted and halved black olives

½ cup sweet (bread and butter) pickles, diced

MARINADE

½ cup vegetable oil

½ cup lemon juice

2 tablespoons cider vinegar

2 tablespoons sugar

1 teaspoon dried dill weed

½ teaspoon salt

⅛ teaspoon black pepper

1. Combine the first five ingredients in a large bowl. Stir in the olives and pickles.

2. Whisk the marinade ingredients together in a bowl or combine them in a bottle and shake to mix. Pour the marinade over the vegetables and stir well. Cover the bowl and refrigerate it for 24 hours, stirring three or four times and shifting the vegetables on the bottom to the top.

3. Adjust the seasonings, adding more sugar or more vinegar to suit your taste for sweet or sour.

4. Drain the vegetables before serving. For a festive look, serve them in a lettuce-lined bowl.

MARY ANN CORRIGAN writes the Five Ingredient Mysteries under the name Maya Corrigan. The first in the series, *By Cook or by Crook*, came out in November 2014.

LISA KING

Eggplant Caprese Salad with Basil Chiffonade and Olive Vinaigrette

The protagonist of my mystery series, Jean Applequist, loves good food and wine but isn't much of a cook. This recipe is perfect for her—easy to make yet deliciously complex. This dish is a smoky, earthy, richer version of the summer caprese salad made from ripe tomatoes, fresh mozzarella, and fresh basil. Smoked mozzarella is available at most supermarkets. Trader Joe's has a lovely version that is semisoft and lightly smoked.

Jean, who is a wine writer, would serve this salad with a medium-weight red wine that is not too high in alcohol, such as cabernet sauvignon, Syrah, zinfandel, rioja, or an Italian Sangiovese-based red such as Chianti. A chilled dry rosé from California, Provence, or Spain would also work nicely.

YIELD: 4 SERVINGS

1 medium eggplant, about 1 pound

¼ cup extra virgin olive oil, plus more for brushing eggplant

Sea salt and freshly ground black pepper, to taste

1 8-ounce ball smoked mozzarella

4 kalamata or other brine-cured black olives, pitted and chopped fine

1 garlic clove, minced

1 tablespoon sherry vinegar (you can substitute red wine vinegar)

6 to 8 large basil leaves

1. Preheat a broiler with a rack placed about 4 inches from the heat. Line a sheet pan with foil.

2. Trim the eggplant and cut it crosswise into ½-inch slices. You should have 8 slices. Brush them on both sides with oil and season lightly with salt and pepper.

3. Put the slices in one layer on the foil-covered sheet pan and broil until browned and tender, turning once and moving slices around to ensure even cooking. (You can also grill the eggplant over medium coals.) Let cool to room temperature.

4. Arrange the eggplant slices on a platter. Trim the rounded ends from the smoked mozzarella ball and cut it crosswise into 8 slices. Put one on each eggplant slice.

5. Make the vinaigrette: Put the olives, garlic, and vinegar in a small bowl. Whisk in the olive oil and season with salt and pepper.

6. Make the basil chiffonade: Stack the basil leaves on a cutting board and roll up the long way. Slice the rolled-up basil into thin strips.

7. Scatter the basil chiffonade over the eggplant and mozzarella. Stir the vinaigrette and spoon it over the salad.

8. Serve at room temperature, accompanied by any remaining vinaigrette.

LISA KING is the author of *Death in a Wine Dark Sea* and *Vulture au Vin*, both featuring wine writer and amateur sleuth Jean Applequist. Lisa is a wine geek and avid home cook.

MO WALSH

Mistaken Potato Salad

The first time I made homemade potato salad, I misread the recipe and made several mistakes—but we liked it better than the correct version I made the next time. Over the years, I've played around with proportions and seasonings and started peeling and dicing the potatoes while warm and heating the dressing mixture to bring out the flavors we like best. This version has a nice bite to it and less mayonnaise than standard potato salad.

YIELD: 20–24 HALF-CUP SERVINGS

DRESSING
4 teaspoons olive oil

4 teaspoons salad oil (such as vegetable oil)

4 teaspoons white vinegar

4 teaspoons lemon juice

Rounded 1/4 teaspoon salt

Rounded 1/4 teaspoon dry mustard

Rounded 1/4 teaspoon paprika

SALAD
Approximately 4 1/2 teaspoons salt, divided

5 pounds unpeeled potatoes

1/2 to 3/4 cup finely chopped onion

1/4 teaspoon ground black pepper

1 to 1 1/2 cups mayonnaise (Hellman's Light)

1 cup chopped celery

5 hard-boiled eggs

1. Prepare Mistaken Dressing: Mix ingredients in a lidded container. Seal and shake well to blend. Set aside.

2. In large saucepan or stockpot, bring a 1-inch depth of salted water to a boil (use 1/2 teaspoon salt per 1 cup water). Add potatoes. Cover and boil for 30 minutes. Drain.

3. For best flavor, peel and cube potatoes while still hot and place in a large stockpot or container with a lid. Use a wide, sturdy spoon or pancake spatula to mix in onion, 2 teaspoons salt, and pepper.

4. Microwave Mistaken Dressing for about 30 seconds. Do not boil. Cover and shake dressing to blend. Pour over potato mixture. Gently turn mixture to coat all potatoes. Cover tightly with lid or plastic wrap and refrigerate for at least 2 hours.

5. Gently stir cold potato mixture to absorb any liquid at the bottom of the container. Add 1 cup mayonnaise and stir to coat potatoes. Add additional mayonnaise to taste, stirring to coat.

6. Gently mix in chopped celery and hard-boiled eggs.

MO WALSH has published crime fiction in *Mary Higgins Clark Mystery Magazine*, *Woman's World*, and five anthologies of Best New England Crime Stories. She is a coauthor of the killer trivia book *A Miscellany of Murder*. Mo is a Derringer Award finalist and Mary Higgins Clark Short Mystery/Suspense Award winner.

CHAPTER FOUR

She sat sat across the table, upright and serious. Her hands were small, much like the rest of her, and restless. She tapped her cigarette. "Listen," she said, "I've nowhere else to turn. I need help, and I need to know how to roast a chicken."

MODEL 1

DAVID MORRELL
Thomas De Quincey's Pasta-Less Pasta

Thomas De Quincey, the main character of my Victorian mystery/thriller, *Murder as a Fine Art*, has a significant place in crime fiction. He invented the true-crime genre with his blood-soaked postscript to *On Murder Considered as One of the Fine Arts*. He influenced Edgar Allan Poe, who in turn inspired Sir Arthur Conan Doyle to create Sherlock Holmes. He wrote the first book about drug addiction, *Confessions of an English Opium-Eater*, quotations from which solve the mystery in what is often called the first detective novel, Wilkie Collins's *The Moonstone*. De Quincey also invented the term *subconscious* and anticipated Freud's theories by more than half a century.

Despite the title of De Quincey's notorious book, he didn't eat opium so much as drink it in the form of laudanum, a mixture of alcohol and powdered opium that was in most medicine cabinets of the Victorian era. The majority of people used laudanum sparingly. The recommended dosage was 3 drops for infants and 20 drops for adults, but De Quincey, by his own estimation, often consumed 1,000 drops per day. At the height of his addiction, his daily intake was 16 ounces.

There were several consequences. On the plus side, opium caused De Quincey to have epical nightmares, which formed the basis of his revolutionary theory about the chambers within chambers of the mind. On the negative side, the strain of trying to control his addiction racked his body with "writhing, throbbing, and palpitating" and made his stomach feel as if rats gnawed it. He tolerated only a few foods. Mostly he subsisted on biscuits and tea or else bread soaked in warm milk.

Pasta would have been unknown to De Quincey. Even if it had been available in Victorian England, its heaviness would probably have made it difficult for him to digest. Given his opium intake, his thoughts were amazingly coherent, indeed brilliant. A gluten reaction might have been all that was necessary to tip the balance and cloud his mind.

Here, then, is a pasta-less pasta that might have sustained Thomas De Quincey and kept his stomach from feeling that it harbored creatures. Its main ingredient is zucchini. This is one of my favorite dishes. It's not only delicious. It's also simple.

YIELD: 2–4 SERVINGS

6 to 10 tender zucchini
2 tablespoons olive oil
Tomato sauce, to taste
Meatballs, to serve
  (optional)

1. Cut the ends off each zucchini; use a potato peeler to cut the zucchini into long, thin ribbons.

2. Place the ribbons in a bowl; toss with olive oil.

3. Sauté the ribbons in a skillet until they are crisp/tender.

4. Add your favorite tomato sauce and meatballs if you like.

Note: This is especially tasty with barbecued chicken.

DAVID MORRELL wrote *First Blood*, the acclaimed novel in which Rambo was created. His numerous best sellers include the classic spy novel *The Brotherhood of the Rose* (the basis for the only television miniseries broadcast after a Super Bowl). An Edgar, Anthony, and Macavity nominee, he received ITW's prestigious Thriller Master award.

LORENZO CARCATERRA

Grandma Maria's Pasta Puttanesca
(PASTA À LA WHORE)

I met Grandma Maria in the summer of 1968 on the island of Ischia, off the coast of Naples. She was dressed in widow's black, the pockets of her dress crammed with candy. She drank strong espresso during the day and in the evenings switched to wine.

World War II had cost Grandma a son and a grandson. She spent five years making the daily trek by boat to Naples to secure what food she could from the black market.

One day I told her I wanted to be a writer.

"What does a writer do?" she asked.

"He tells stories," I said.

"Like the ones in the books you read?"

"Those are great stories," I said. "I don't have any of those."

"Life gives you all the stories you need," she said.

One night, joined by my cousin Paolo, we sat and ate Grandma's pasta puttanesca.

"I see Patricia is among your group of friends," she said. "I am friends with her mother and father."

"I met her sisters the other day," I said. "They are much older."

Grandma nodded. "During the war, her father was in the army. Years went by and her mother had no word from him. Then one day she got a letter back. It said that her husband was dead. She had no money and there were children to feed. The Nazis had taken over the island. It was said she spent time with soldiers, earned money for what she did, and with that paid for black market supplies."

Grandma sipped her wine. "The war ends, the Nazis and the Americans leave. Six months later, her husband returns. He had been in a prison camp in Africa. It wasn't long before he was told what his wife had done. He went to see a priest and your grandfather to ask for advice."

"What did they tell him?" Paolo asked.

"That he was young and would meet another woman. Maybe fall in love. But how would he know, they asked, what this woman did during the war? They told him what his wife had done had kept his children alive."

"So they stayed together?" I said.

She nodded. "They slept apart for a few years and then, with time, they became what they were meant to be and Patricia was born. You see them now, walk arm in arm, as happy as when they were young."

Grandma looked at me. "Was the story as good as the ones in your books?" she asked.

"Yes," I said.

She rested her hand on mine. "Then I could be a writer, no?"

"Yes, Nonna," I said.

"And if I can be a writer," she said, "you can be, too. That story belongs to you now."

YIELD: 3–4 SERVINGS FOR BIG EATERS; 5–6 FOR PORTION-CONTROL EATERS (IN OTHER WORDS, NOT ANY MEMBERS OF MY FAMILY)

SAUCE

(You can substitute 1 32-ounce jar marinara sauce, such as Rao's, instead of making from scratch)

2 cloves garlic

½ cup extra virgin olive oil

1 large can San Marzano tomatoes

2 tablespoons chopped fresh oregano (Grandma Maria believed there was no such thing as too much oregano)

8 fresh basil leaves, chopped

1 tablespoon of the juice from a jar of hot cherry peppers

¼ to ½ cup red wine

1 teaspoon salt

PASTA

21 pitted kalamata olives, quartered

7 anchovies, cut into slivers

¼ to ½ cup capers with their juice

½ teaspoon crushed red pepper flakes, or to taste

1 pound spaghetti or linguine

1. Make the sauce, or if you're using canned sauce, skip to step 4. Cut garlic cloves in half and flatten them with either the palm of your hand or the base of a knife. Sauté in olive oil until garlic turns light brown.

2. Add tomatoes, herbs, and hot cherry pepper juice and bring to low boil.

3. Add wine and simmer over very low heat for 30 to 60 minutes. (You can either remove the garlic or leave in the sauce. Grandma liked her garlic so it stayed.) When it has been cooking for at least 20 minutes, taste the sauce and add the salt and more spice if necessary.

4. Meanwhile, fill a pasta pot with water and bring to a low boil.

5. Okay, the sauce is cooking; the pasta water is on the stove, and you are now ready to make your puttanesca: Add the olives (Grandma loved them, so that's why she went heavy on them), anchovies, capers with their liquid, and red pepper to the sauce. Let the sauce cook for 5 more minutes.

6. Turn your water up to a rolling boil. Toss in the pasta. (Grandma liked spaghetti. I like linguini.) Cook according to the package directions (less time for al dente). Do not add oil or salt to the water—that would drive Grandma Maria to drink. When the pasta is cooked, drain in a colander.

7. Ladle three large scoops of sauce into the empty pasta pot. Toss the pasta back into the pot and pour the rest of sauce on top of the pasta. Stir sauce and pasta together. Serve with a loaf of fresh Italian bread, a bottle of red wine, a bottle of mineral water—and a CD of Neapolitan folk songs playing in the background.

LORENZO CARCATERRA is the #1 *New York Times* best-selling author of *Sleepers*, *A Safe Place*, *Apaches*, *Gangster*, *Street Boys*, *Paradise City*, *Midnight Angels*, and *The Wolf*. He was writer/producer for *Law & Order*. He has written for *National Geographic Traveler*, the *New York Times Sunday Magazine*, and *Details*. He lives with Gus, an Olde English Bulldogge.

LESLIE BUDEWITZ

Farfalle with Fennel and Pine Nuts

I was not born into a foodie family. But I was born into a storytelling family. I loved to linger at the table while my father, a traveling salesman who was gone most weekdays, told his stories. My mother often paused while cleaning up to lean against the kitchen counter and listen.

Food is still story to me. I write traditional or "cozy" mysteries, where the focus is as much on the characters and their lives as on the puzzle of who killed whom and why. My Food Lovers' Village Mysteries are set in Jewel Bay, Montana, a lakeside resort community on the road to Glacier National Park—a town that calls itself a "Food Lovers' Village." Erin Murphy, my main character, is the thirty-two-year-old manager of the Merc, a market specializing in regional foods, located in her family's century-old building that once held the town's original grocery. Erin has a passion for pasta, retail, and huckleberry chocolates—and an unexpected talent for solving murder.

Unlike me, Erin did grow up in a food-loving family. She's half Irish, half Italian. Her mother Francesca—aka Fresca—makes the fresh pasta, sauces, and pestos that Merc customers love. The series begins with *Death al Dente*—or murder not quite well-done—set at an Italian food festival Erin cooks up to kick off summer. Murder is not the only crime—or the only mystery. Erin thinks that if she can figure out who's been spreading the rumors that Fresca stole the recipes she used to build her business, she'll be closer to identifying the killer. She finds a clue in a handwritten recipe card.

In every book, I get to explore food along with the mystery. It's a natural combination to me. Murder is stressful, and who doesn't eat when stressed? But more importantly, murder is unnatural. It damages the threads that tie a community together. The killer must be brought to justice and the social order restored.

And what does that better than food?

YIELD: 4–6 SERVINGS AS A MAIN COURSE; 6–8 SERVINGS AS A SIDE DISH

½ cup pine nuts

¼ cup olive oil

1 medium onion, chopped

1½ pounds fennel bulb

½ cup raisins—dark, golden, or a mix

1 teaspoon salt

¼ teaspoon ground cinnamon

1. Toast the pine nuts at 300°F until lightly browned, about 10 minutes. (Don't wait until the nuts look dark, as they will continue cooking after being removed from the oven.) Set aside.

2. Heat the oil in a large saucepan. Add the onions and sauté until they begin to turn golden.

3. While the onions are cooking, prepare the fennel by removing the green stems and fronds. Chop and reserve about 2 tablespoons of fronds for garnish; set aside. Discard the stems. Remove any blemished or tough layers of the bulb and trim a thin slice from the base. Cut the bulb in half lengthwise through the base. Lay each half cut side down and slice thinly.

½ cup cold water

¾ pound farfalle
  (bow tie pasta)

OPTIONAL
ADDITIONS

½ cup grated Parmesan
  cheese

OR

1 cup halved cherry or
  grape tomatoes

1 cup chopped canned
  artichokes (not
  marinated)

1 cup crumbled
  goat cheese

4. When the onions soften and begin to turn golden, add the fennel, raisins, salt, cinnamon, and cold water to the pan. Stir, cover, and cook over medium heat for 15 to 20 minutes, or until the fennel softens.

5. While the fennel mixture is cooking, cook and drain the pasta. Toss the hot pasta with the fennel mixture and add the toasted pine nuts. Stir in grated Parmesan or tomatoes, artichokes, and goat cheese. Mix well.

6. Garnish with chopped fennel fronds and serve.

Note: This dish is particularly good served with grilled chicken or shrimp.

LESLIE BUDEWITZ is the author of the Food Lovers' Village Mysteries. The latest, *Crime Rib*, was published in July 2014. The first, *Death al Dente*, won the 2013 Agatha Award for Best First Novel. Leslie's guide for writers, *Books, Crooks and Counselors: How to Write Accurately about Criminal Law and Courtroom Procedure* (Quill Driver Books), won the 2011 Agatha Award for Best Nonfiction. Her website is lesliebudewitz.com.

RAYMOND BENSON

Zillion Calorie Mac and Cheese

This is a recipe of my mother's to which I have added tons of extra calories. I remember having it as a regular dish on Thanksgiving, but it's good anytime. Okay, it's comfort food. It's fattening, but it's delicious, so who cares?

I'd like to tie it in to my writing, but this recipe has nothing to do with the Black Stiletto, James Bond, my novelizations of video games and other media franchises, or my stand-alone thrillers. But perhaps you could settle down with the latest Black Stiletto installment and stuff yourself with my mac and cheese. And maybe some red wine. I may be biased, but *that* is tying the dish into my writing.

YIELD: 4 SERVINGS

1 8-ounce box macaroni

3 tablespoons flour

3 tablespoons butter

2 cups milk

¼ teaspoon salt

¼ teaspoon black pepper

12 or more slices from a 16-slice pack of Kraft Deli Deluxe American cheese slices (When I was a kid, it used to come in a block that you could slice from, but now you have to settle for sandwich slice packs.)

1. Preheat oven to 350°F. Grease a casserole pan.

2. Bring a large pot of water to a boil. Cook macaroni according to package instructions.

3. Mix flour, butter, milk, salt, and pepper in a saucepan. Heat on low, stirring frequently. As the mixture becomes hot, drop in slices of cheese one at a time and stir until melted. Repeat until 12 slices have been added. Add more cheese if you're really a glutton for cheesiness.

4. Drain macaroni and pour it into a greased casserole pan. Then pour in the hot cheesy mixture. Stir until macaroni is evenly distributed. Shred any remaining cheese slices on top of casserole. Cover with foil and bake for 20 minutes.

5. Remove foil and bake uncovered for 5 to 10 minutes more, watching to make sure the top doesn't get too brown.

6. Pig out.

RAYMOND BENSON is the author of more than thirty published titles. His latest thrillers are the Black Stiletto books, the most recent of which is *The Black Stiletto: Endings & Beginnings*. He's also known for being the first American author to write official James Bond novels. Find out more at raymondbenson.com.

JOELLE CHARBONNEAU
Testing Pizza

The Testing trilogy takes place one hundred years after a world war poisoned the earth's soil and water supply with biological and chemical weapons. Since that time, the leaders of the United Commonwealth (chosen through a process known as the Testing) have had to find ways to cleanse the earth and make things grow and thrive again. While they have had success, they haven't been able to restore things completely. My heroine, Cia Vale, and other aspiring future leaders are working on that. But a lot of the recipes available today wouldn't work in Cia's world.

However, like any good society, they do have pizza. After the first round of Testing, Cia and her friends are served pizza for dinner. Since pizza is a personal favorite of mine (because who doesn't like pizza?), I decided to create a recipe that would be possible to make in *The Testing*.

YIELD: 1 10-TO-12-INCH PIZZA

¼ ounce dry active yeast—best obtained from the local biological engineer

1 teaspoon granulated sugar (if sugar is available in your colony)

1 cup warm (treated so it is safe to drink) water

2½ cups flour

2 tablespoons oil (rendered animal fat will do if your colony doesn't have means to produce oil), plus more for topping

1 teaspoon salt (if salt is not available, just ignore this)

3 to 4 large tomatoes, preferably genetically enhanced, thinly sliced

2 garlic cloves, minced

3 to 4 basil leaves

4 ounces sliced white cheese

1. Preheat oven to 450°F (you can also cook the pizza in a hot open wood oven, depending on your colony's power allotment). In a bowl, dissolve yeast, sugar, and water and let stand for about 10 minutes.

2. Stir flour, oil, and salt (if you have it) into yeast mixture until smooth. Let rest for 5 minutes.

3. Turn dough onto a lightly floured surface and pat or roll it until flat. Whatever shape of pan you have would be the shape you want to roll it into.

4. Lightly grease the pan and then dust it with cornmeal, if available (Madison colony has done great work with genetically resequencing corn and has been able to consistently provide good harvests). Place dough on pan.

5. Lightly coat the dough with olive oil (or whatever oil or fat you have). Lay tomatoes on the pizza crust, followed by garlic and basil leaves. Place slices of cheese on top.

6. Bake for 15 to 20 minutes or until golden brown. Yummy!

JOELLE CHARBONNEAU has performed in musical productions across Chicagoland. She teaches voice lessons and is the author of the *New York Times* best-selling Testing trilogy (*The Testing*, *Independent Study*, and *Graduation Day*), the Rebecca Robbins mysteries (Minotaur Books), and the Glee Club mysteries (Berkley).

SUE GRAFTON

Kinsey Millhone's Famous Peanut Butter & Pickle Sandwich

I've received letters from readers who are completely aghast at the notion of eating this culinary wonder. Others actually try it despite their misgivings. Once recovered, these same readers confess that it's not half bad. Strangely yummy, they say. Some take a jauntier attitude and begin to try improvements, which Kinsey and I are quick to discourage.

I should point out that Kinsey eats more of these than I do since she's (almost) entirely fictional and doesn't gain weight.

The following is the actual, true, uncensored recipe.

YIELD: 1 SANDWICH

Jif Extra Crunchy Peanut Butter (no substitutions, please)

2 slices Health-Nut Bread, or some whole grain equivalent

6 or 7 Vlasic Bread & Butter Chips (again, no substitutions or we can't be responsible for the results)

1. Spread gobs of the peanut butter on one slice of bread

2. Place bread and butter chips on the peanut butter.

3. Top with second slice of bread and cut on the diagonal.

SUE GRAFTON is the author of twenty-two detective novels featuring private eye Kinsey Millhone.

KEN LUDWIG

Lenore Schneiderman's Gourmet Quiche

My play, *The Game's Afoot,* which won the 2012 Edgar Award for Best Play, concerns William Gillette, the actor who wrote the play *Sherlock Holmes* with Arthur Conan Doyle's approval—and then starred in it on Broadway and around the world for the next thirty years. This quiche Provençal (from a recipe by dear friend Lenore Schneiderman) is just the kind of dish that Gillette would have served to his extravagant Broadway guests at Gillette Castle when they came upriver from New York City for a weekend of good food, games, and revelry.

Not only does the dish require the kind of Holmesian precision that Gillette worshipped, but, as in *The Game's Afoot,* a séance will undoubtedly confirm Gillette's taste in the matter. So please, by all means, gather round the dining room table, join hands, and channel Arthur Conan Doyle, William Gillette, and Sherlock Holmes—and they will all assure you that this quiche Provençal is their favorite dish for a mysterious weekend party.

Enjoy!

YIELD: 6–8 SERVINGS

1 medium onion, sliced

½ cup chopped green pepper

2 tablespoons vegetable oil

2 medium tomatoes, cut into small wedges

1 cup thinly sliced zucchini

1 tablespoon chopped parsley

½ teaspoon garlic salt

Salt and black pepper, to taste

1 unbaked 9-inch pie shell

6 eggs, well beaten

1¼ cups light cream or half-and-half

1. Preheat oven to 425°F.

2. Sauté the onions and green peppers in vegetable oil in a skillet until onions are soft. Add the tomatoes, zucchini, parsley, and seasonings. Cook uncovered for 10 minutes, stirring frequently.

3. Bake the pie shell for 5 minutes. Remove from the oven and lower oven temperature to 350°F.

4. Combine eggs and cream (or half-and-half). Pour into pie shell. Spoon in vegetable mixture.

5. Bake for 30 to 35 minutes, or until a knife inserted in the center comes out clean.

KEN LUDWIG is an internationally acclaimed playwright whose numerous hits on Broadway include *Lend Me a Tenor* and *Crazy for You.* His work has been performed in more than thirty countries in over twenty languages, and his book *How to Teach Your Children Shakespeare* is published by Random House. For more information, visit kenludwig.com.

DIANNE EMLEY

Croque Madame Californienne

This is a lighter version of the classic French baked sandwich, which I created to use the bounty of tomatoes and basil from my California summer garden. It can be served as an easy entrée with a side salad or cut into squares and served as an appetizer. Homicide detective Nan Vining, my series lead, would enjoy this meal at the table of her boyfriend, Detective Jim Kissick. Nan's not much for cooking or gardening, but Jim loves cooking and he loves Nan.

YIELD: 6 SERVINGS

About half a loaf of day-old French bread, enough to cut 12 ½-inch slices

½ pound grated Gruyère or Jarlsberg cheese, divided

½ large sweet onion (such as Vidalia or Maui), sliced paper-thin

3 to 4 large tomatoes (any type), halved, seeded, and sliced ¼ inch thick

1 garlic clove, sliced paper-thin

½ cup fresh basil leaves, torn (mix sweet basil, black opal, or any type)

1 tablespoon extra virgin olive oil

1 tablespoon capers

1. Preheat oven to 400°F. Oil an 8-inch square baking dish.

2. Place the bread in a single layer to cover the bottom of the dish. Sprinkle half the cheese over the bread. Layer the onion slices and the tomatoes over the onions. Layer the garlic slices over the tomatoes. Evenly sprinkle the torn basil leaves over the garlic.

3. Drizzle the olive oil lightly over the top. Sprinkle the remaining cheese on top, leaving a few openings to let the tomatoes show (looks nice). Sprinkle the capers over the top layer of cheese.

4. Bake uncovered for 15 minutes. Turn the oven to broil and broil for 2 to 3 minutes, or until cheese browns.

5. Let stand for 5 or 10 minutes before serving.

Note: You may add a layer of ham (this makes it a Croque Monsieur), or try it with leftover chicken.

DIANNE EMLEY is the *Los Angeles Times* best-selling author of the Detective Nan Vining Thrillers and the Iris Thorne Mysteries. Her stand-alone paranormal mystery, *The Night Visitor*, is published by Alibi/Random House. An L.A. native, she lives with her husband in the Central California wine country.

ALAN ORLOFF

Killer Tofu

Many people don't like tofu. I should know; I used to be one of them. But a few years back, on an "eat healthier" kick, I figured I'd give it a whirl. In order to make it palatable, though, I had to invent my own recipe. After an ill-advised experiment involving tofu, hot fudge sauce, bananas, and maraschino cherries, I finally came up with a dish I liked.

I call this recipe Killer Tofu, in support of my first Channing Hayes book, *Killer Routine* (see the resemblance?). Of course, the protagonist in that book, Channing Hayes, wouldn't eat tofu if it were the last thing in his neighbor's fridge. (Being a comedian, he's more partial to sugary breakfast cereals with cartoon character mascots.)

Believe it or not, this is a dish I sometimes serve at Thanksgiving!

YIELD: 6 SERVINGS

2 tablespoons canola oil

1 small onion, diced

1 green or red pepper, diced (optional)

1 1-pound block extra firm tofu, rinsed and diced

½ pound frozen corn kernels, give or take

¼ cup mustard

¼ cup ketchup

¼ cup barbecue sauce

3 tablespoons hot sauce (like sriracha), or to taste

1. Heat oil in a wok or large skillet.

2. Stir-fry onion (and pepper, if you're using it) on high heat for about 2 minutes.

3. Add tofu and stir-fry for another minute.

4. Add corn, mustard, ketchup, barbecue sauce, and hot sauce, stirring well.

5. Cook until everything's nice and hot, about 5 more minutes.

ALAN ORLOFF's debut mystery, *Diamonds for the Dead*, was a 2010 Agatha Award finalist for Best First Novel. He has written two books in the Last Laff mystery series, *Killer Routine* and *Deadly Campaign*, and writing as Zak Allen, he has published *The Taste*, *First Time Killer*, and *Ride-Along*. Visit alanorloff.com.

FELIX FRANCIS
Beef Stroganoff

One of my favorite meals is beef stroganoff, and I put it in one of my books. The recipe is as follows, as made by the chef Max Moreton, the lead character in *Dead Heat*.

YIELD: 2 SERVINGS

½ pound beef tenderloin

Salt and black pepper, to taste

Olive oil for frying

1 medium red onion, sliced

2 handfuls wild mushrooms, sliced

A little plain flour

A generous measure of brandy

⅓ cup sour cream

1 tablespoon freshly squeezed lemon juice

1 teaspoon paprika

1 large potato, peeled

½ garlic clove, chopped (if desired)

FROM *DEAD HEAT*:

I trimmed the beef and cut it into strips before seasoning and then searing it in a hot frying pan. Then I fried a sliced onion and some mushrooms until they were tender and added them to the beef with some plain flour. I poured a generous measure of cognac over the mixture and, much to Caroline's horror, flamed off the alcohol.

"You'll set the whole bloody building on fire," Caroline shouted as the flames leaped towards her ceiling, and I laughed.

Next I carefully poured in some sour cream and a small amount of lemon juice, and sprinkled some paprika over the top. I had previously taken a large potato and, as Caroline didn't have a kitchen mandolin, I had grated it on the large-hole side of her box cheese grater to produce long thin strips of potato that I now fried briefly in a deep fryer to produce crisp brown potato straws, while my beef mixture warmed on a low heat.

"I thought beef stroganoff was served with rice," she said, watching me. "And I didn't expect a chef to use my deep-fat fryer."

"I use one all the time," I said. "I know that fried food is not considered very healthy but it tastes so good, and it's fine if you eat it only in moderation and use the right oil for the frying. . . ." I lifted the basket of potato straws out of the oil. "It's traditional in Russia to serve beef stroganoff with potato straws, although lots of people like serving it with rice."

We sat together on the sofa in her sitting room and ate off trays on our laps.

"Not bad," she said. "Why is it called stroganoff?"

"After the Russian who invented it, I think. . . ."

"It's nice." She took another forkful. "What gives it such a distinctive flavor?" she asked with her mouth full.

"The sour cream and the paprika," I said, laughing. "This dish used to be on lots of restaurant menus, but, unfortunately, these days it tends to be made without the beef, is called mushroom stroganoff and is served up for vegetarians."

FELIX FRANCIS is the younger son of literary legend, MWA Grand Master, and three-time Edgar winner Dick Francis. Felix has taken over the writing of the Dick Francis novels and has recently finished *Damage*, his ninth, which was published in October 2014. Felix lives in England with his wife, Debbie.

GILLIAN FLYNN

Beef Skillet Fiesta

Be warned: I am no gourmet. I come from a long, proud Midwestern tradition of meals made from snack chips and canned soup. My characters tend to follow suit: They like their food simple and tasty. So here's my favorite stove-top recipe, Beef Skillet Fiesta, which my mom cooked for her family and I now cook for mine.

YIELD: 4 SERVINGS

1 pound ground beef

¼ cup diced onion

2 teaspoons salt

1 teaspoon chili powder

¼ teaspoon black pepper

1 16-ounce can diced tomatoes

1 12-ounce can corn

1¼ cups beef bouillon

½ cup thin strips of green pepper

1⅓ cups Minute rice

1. Brown ground beef in a skillet and drain. Add onion and cook until tender.

2. Add salt, chili powder, pepper, tomatoes, corn, and bouillon and bring to a boil. Stir in green pepper. Bring to a boil again.

3. Stir in rice, remove from heat, and cover. Let stand for 5 minutes.

4. Fluff with a fork.

5. Serve with cottage cheese. (The cottage cheese part isn't strictly required, but highly recommended—cottage cheese makes everything better.)

Note: If you prefer regular rice to Minute rice, cook the rice separately and spoon the Skillet Fiesta over it.

GILLIAN FLYNN is the author of the #1 *New York Times* best seller *Gone Girl*, the *New York Times* best seller *Dark Places*, and the Dagger Award–winning *Sharp Objects*. She is also the screenwriter for the film adaptation of *Gone Girl*, directed by David Fincher and starring Ben Affleck.

GREG HERREN

Greg's New Orleans Slow-Cooker Meatballs

The only thing I might love more than writing is cooking, but as someone who now juggles a full-time day job, editing manuscripts, and writing my own books—in addition to any number of other hobbies and interests—finding the time to cook isn't always easy. And I think every writer can identify with getting so lost in your manuscript that suddenly it's dinnertime and you haven't even thought about what to make.

This recipe is wonderful—it's something I've played around with for years, tinkering with ingredients and what to serve with it. These meatballs and the gravy are incredibly versatile, which really comes in handy when you're writing. The prep work doesn't take all that long—I always dice the peppers and onions and celery while I'm browning the meatballs so I can just add everything into the slow cooker at the same time. It doesn't even need to be stirred more than once or twice—I generally do that when I am taking a break from the computer to get something to drink or go to the bathroom. The meatballs can be served over egg noodles, rice, or mashed potatoes; I've even baked potatoes to go with them, using the gravy to flavor the potatoes. That versatility means you can have them three or more nights in a row without really getting tired of them—and the flavor gets stronger each day. So for a little less than an hour of prep work you can alleviate your need to cook anything for several days—more time for writing, and no need to revert to peanut butter sandwiches!

What really finished the recipe for me was the spices and the cooking sherry. I had just finished writing my third Scotty Bradley mystery, *Mardi Gras Mambo*, and was doing some research for the next, which was going to be built around a New Orleans restaurant (fictional, of course). While researching in the kitchen of a major restaurant, I noticed the use of four spices I'd never really seen combined before; it struck me as odd, but when I questioned the chef, he just smiled and let me taste the sauce. It blew my socks off—and I mused out loud that I should add them to my meatball recipe. He nodded gravely and told me to also add cooking sherry. That very weekend, I did—and I haven't altered the recipe since!

I never wrote the restaurant mystery . . . but maybe I should! And I think I need to make these meatballs again—it's been way too long!

YIELD: 6–8 SERVINGS, DEPENDING ON THE APPETITE

1 pound ground pork
1 pound lean ground sirloin
½ cup milk
½ cup bread crumbs

1. Combine the pork and the sirloin in a bowl. Add the milk and the breadcrumbs and mix by hand. Once the meat is thoroughly mixed, roll into ½-inch-wide balls. Brown on each side in a skillet over medium heat, and then remove to a paper towel. Pat them dry with another paper towel.

2. In a slow cooker, combine the rest of the ingredients except for the mushrooms and whisk until smooth. Add the meatballs, and then cook for 7 hours on low.

2 cans French onion soup

2 cans cream of mushroom soup

1 cup cooking sherry

1 cup diced onions

1 cup diced bell pepper

1 cup diced celery

2 bay leaves

1 tablespoon each salt, black pepper, white pepper, cayenne pepper, basil, minced garlic, and thyme

½ cup diced jalapeños

2 cups sliced mushrooms

3. Add the mushrooms and check the thickness of the gravy. If it isn't thick enough, mix 2 tablespoons flour into 1 cup of water until smooth. Add it to the gravy and stir until it thickens. If it's still not thick enough, repeat the process one more time. The additional water won't affect the flavor of the gravy.

4. Cook for 1 hour more on low.

Note: You can serve this as a stew, or over rice or egg noodles or mashed potatoes. Store whatever's left over in the refrigerator in a plastic container—and the longer it sits in the refrigerator, the more flavorful the meatballs become.

VARIATIONS

If you like your food less spicy, halve the cayenne and leave out the jalapeños.

You can also add carrots and cut-up potatoes, if you want it to be more of a stew. Just make sure you do this at the beginning, so they can cook thoroughly.

GREG HERREN is the award-winning author of almost thirty novels and more than fifty short stories. He currently lives and cooks in the Lower Garden District of New Orleans.

CHARLAINE HARRIS

Charlaine's Very Unsophisticated Supper Dip

This recipe is very good to make after a day spent working on something tense and finicky. It is simple, requires about 10 minutes to assemble, and after that you just let it simmer until you're ready to eat, though you do have to stir it from time to time and add more wine if necessary.

YIELD: 5 SERVINGS

2 pounds ground chicken (or beef)

¾ cup chopped onion

2 tablespoons chili powder, or more to taste

1 package dry ranch dressing mix

½ cup taco seasoning

2 15½-ounce cans charro beans, undrained

1 15½-ounce can black beans, drained

1 15½-ounce can Ro-Tel diced tomatoes and green chilies

1 6-ounce can tomato paste

8 ounces tomato sauce

1 cup red wine

To serve: shredded cheddar or Monterey Jack cheese and your favorite sturdy tortilla chips

1. Brown the meat in a deep skillet with the chopped onion, and sprinkle generously with chili powder.

2. Transfer the meat mixture into a 3-quart pan with the rest of the ingredients except cheese and tortilla chips.

3. Cover the pan. Let this all simmer gently together for at least an hour. Stir occasionally, and add more wine or tomato sauce if it gets too thick.

4. Serve in bowls. Sprinkle generously with cheese. Scoop up with tortilla chips.

CHARLAINE HARRIS, whose most recent book is *Midnight Crossroad*, alternates between cooking whatever's easy and planning a whole menu. The older she gets, the more "easy" wins. Charlaine has a husband, three grown children, two grandchildren, and a passel of dogs. She has been a professional writer for thirty-five years. She lives on a cliff in Texas.

KARIN SLAUGHTER

Cathy's Coke Roast

My grandmother Cathy taught me how to make this dish, which, she insisted, "even an idiot can do." And she was right! It's my signature dish. Any Southerner will tell you that Coke is a fantastic tenderizer (it also cleans soap scum, but we are talking about meat here).

YIELD: 4–6 SERVINGS

3 pounds organic beef roast

Ground black pepper, to taste

1 2-liter bottle Coca-Cola

2 bay leaves

1 cup beef broth

1 cup baby carrots

1 cup sliced mushrooms

1 cup diced onion

2 stalks celery, diced

4 red potatoes, sliced

1 cup green beans, snapped and cut in half

Pinch dried parsley, or to taste

Pinch dried basil, or to taste

1. Place roast in a large bowl and sprinkle with pepper. Pour Coke over the roast until nearly covered. Add the bay leaves. Cover roast and let sit in fridge overnight.

2. The next day, drain Coke and place roast in a slow cooker. Add beef broth and all vegetables. Season with pepper, parsley, and basil. Cook on high for 3 hours.

3. Set the slow cooker on low and cook for an additional 3 hours.

KARIN SLAUGHTER is the *New York Times* best-selling and Edgar Award–winning author author of *Cop Town* and thirteen other novels that have sold over thirty million copies in thirty-two languages. Karin's books have debuted at #1 in the United Kingdom, Germany, and the Netherlands. A long-time resident of Atlanta, she splits her time between the kitchen and the living room.

KATE COLLINS

Spicy Joes

My recipe is an Americanized version of a Greek recipe that my husband, a full-blooded Greek, loved. Since I've never been a lamb fan, I switched out the meat and added a lot of zip. It became one of our favorite dishes, something I could make quickly after a long afternoon at the computer. It's also great to serve when guests stop by unexpectedly. In honor of my beloved Greek, here is my version of Mediterranean-style sloppy joes.

YIELD: 4 SERVINGS

1 small onion, diced

1 tablespoon olive oil

2 teaspoons ground allspice

2 teaspoons ground cinnamon

½ teaspoon crushed red pepper flakes (or more if you like it hot)

¼ teaspoon ground black pepper

¼ teaspoon sea salt, or to taste

2 teaspoons smoked paprika

1 tablespoon parsley (optional)

2 teaspoons turmeric (optional)

1 pound ground beef (chuck, if possible)

¼ to ⅓ cup ketchup

1. In a deep skillet, sauté onion in olive oil over medium heat with all spices for about 4 minutes.

2. Add beef and ketchup. Simmer until beef is not pink.

3. Serve on toasted buns or top with hummus.

Note: Spicy Joes can also be made in a slow cooker. Just brown the meat first, combine everything in the slow cooker, and then cook on low heat for 8 to 12 hours. It freezes well, too.

KATE COLLINS is the *New York Times* best-selling author of the popular and long-running Flower Shop Mystery series. *A Root Awakening*, sixteenth in the series, was a February 2015 release. Read about Kate's mysteries, historical romances, and children's anthologies at katecollinsbooks.com.

NANCY J. COHEN

Brisket with Apricot & Prunes

Brisket is a staple of Jewish holidays. You'll find this dish often at Rosh Hashanah and Passover celebrations. Sweet potatoes and prunes may be combined with cooked carrots and honey, as in a side dish known as *tsimmes*, or cooked with the meat as in this dish. Marsala wine is my secret ingredient, not only here but also when I make Swedish meatballs.

The mouthwatering aroma of brisket simmering on the stove brings to mind home-cooked meals and traditional holidays. Marla Shore, the heroine sleuth in my Bad Hair Day series, enjoys keeping up with tradition and cooking these dishes for her extended family, including her non-Jewish fiancé. We'll find her celebrating various holidays throughout the series, from Thanksgiving in *Dead Roots* to Passover in *Hanging by a Hair*. After dealing with murderers and nearly losing her life in each episode, how best to rejoice at being alive than with family and friends over a delicious meal?

YIELD: 6–8 SERVINGS

3½ pounds flat-cut beef brisket

2 tablespoons olive oil

2 medium onions, sliced

1 cup low-sodium beef broth

¼ cup marsala wine

3 tablespoons balsamic vinegar

3 tablespoons honey

½ teaspoon ground ginger

½ teaspoon ground cloves

½ teaspoon ground cinnamon

2 pounds sweet potatoes, peeled and cut into chunks

1 cup pitted prunes

1 cup dried apricots

1. Preheat oven to 350°F. Trim fat off brisket. Heat oil in an ovenproof heavy Dutch oven and add meat, browning on both sides. Remove brisket. Add onions and sauté until wilted, about 5 minutes. Meanwhile, mix beef broth, wine, balsamic vinegar, honey, ginger, cloves, and cinnamon in a bowl.

2. Place brisket on top of onions in pot. Pour broth mixture over meat. Cover, place in oven, and bake for 2 hours.

3. Add sweet potato chunks. Scatter dried fruit on top. Cover and bake for 1 more hour, or until meat is tender.

4. Transfer meat to a cutting board. Spoon out fruit with a slotted spoon. Cut meat thinly across the grain. Serve with fruit and pan juices.

NANCY J. COHEN writes the humorous Bad Hair Day mystery series featuring hairdresser Marla Shore, who solves crimes with wit and style under the sultry South Florida sun. *Hanging by a Hair* is her latest title and eleventh in the series. Visit her website: nancyjcohen.com.

BETH GROUNDWATER

Tarragon-Raspberry Flank Steak with Caramelized Onions, Kale, and Mango Salsa

Beef is a very popular main dish in my home state of Colorado since so many cattle are raised here. However, it doesn't have to be fatty and unhealthy. Flank steak is one of my favorite cuts for its leanness, and this recipe of my own creation adds a lot of vitamin-packed vegetables and fruits. It's easy enough to prepare that it could be served at a riverside campsite after an exciting day of whitewater rafting, such as my river ranger and rafting guide Mandy Tanner does in my Rocky Mountain Outdoor Adventures series.

YIELD: 6 SERVINGS

1 flank steak

2 teaspoons dried tarragon, divided

⅔ cup low-fat raspberry vinaigrette salad dressing

1 ripe mango

1 16-ounce jar chipotle salsa

2 medium onions

1 large bunch fresh kale

2 tablespoons vegetable oil

Salt and black pepper, to taste

1. Sprinkle both sides of flank steak with ½ teaspoon of the tarragon and marinate for 1 to 2 hours in raspberry vinaigrette, turning a few times.

2. Preheat grill. Peel and dice mango, mix with salsa and 1 teaspoon of the tarragon, and set aside.

3. Peel onions, slice in half, then slice halves into ¼-inch slices. Wash kale and tear into large bite-size pieces.

4. Grill flank steak for 5 to 6 minutes per side until medium-rare. While steak is grilling, heat oil over medium heat in a large nonstick skillet. Add onions and stir-fry until golden, about 8 to 10 minutes.

5. Add kale, the remaining ½ teaspoon tarragon, salt, and pepper to skillet. Mix with onions, cover, and lower heat to medium-low. Let steam for about 3 to 5 minutes, until kale is bright green and soft.

6. Let flank steak rest while the kale finishes cooking and you mound onions and kale to one side on each of 6 plates.

7. Slice flank steak thinly on the diagonal and fan 4 slices on each plate, with the mound of kale forming the apex of the fan. Spoon a trail of mango salsa across the tips of the fans. Serve immediately with any leftover salsa on the table.

BETH GROUNDWATER writes the Claire Hanover gift basket designer mystery series and the Rocky Mountain Outdoor Adventures mystery series starring whitewater river ranger Mandy Tanner. Beth enjoys Colorado's many outdoor activities, including skiing and whitewater rafting, and loves talking to book clubs. Please visit her website: bethgroundwater.com.

LOUISE PENNY

Madame Benoît's Tourtière

This recipe for *tourtière* comes from one of our neighbors in the Quebec countryside south of Montreal. Her name was Jehane Benoît, but she was known far and wide simply as Madame Benoît. She compiled the first books of Canadian recipes and popularized Québécoise cuisine. Some rustic, some delicate. All delicious. She was hailed a hero and adored.

She died in 1987 and the road she lived on, not far from us, was renamed Chemin Benoît.

Tourtière is a purely Québécois dish, and each region claims parenthood and makes it slightly differently. Since it is a meat pie, the variations depend on the types of meat raised and hunted in each region. But there are also distinctions in the spices used and even how the meat is cut up. And best not to raise the issue of potatoes.

While eaten year round, tourtière has become associated in Quebec with the huge family celebrations on Christmas Eve and New Year's Eve. Those parties are called *réveillon,* which loosely translates as either "struggling to stay awake past midnight when the food is finally served" or *"Maudit,* I've eaten so much I'm going to explode. But perhaps just one more bite of pie . . ."

I described a Christmas Eve *réveillon* in my book *A Fatal Grace.*

The fire was lit, as were a few of the guests. In the dining room the gate-legged table was open full and groaning with casseroles and tourtières, *homemade molasses-baked beans and maple-cured ham. A turkey sat at the head of the table like a Victorian gentleman. . . .*

Thus did Émilie Longré hold her réveillon, *the party that spanned Christmas Eve and Christmas Day, an old Québécois tradition, just as her mother and* grandmère *had done in this very same home on this very same night.*

Now, choosing a particular tourtière recipe for this cookbook is fraught with difficulty since, as I said, each region genuinely believes it created the first one and therefore the rest are pretenders and probably inedible. Perhaps even poison.

In an attempt to side-step this culinary grenade, I've chosen Madame Benoît's recipe, and I hope my Québécois compatriots elsewhere in the province will understand my loyalty to a remarkable neighbor.

YIELD: 1 9-INCH PIE

1 pound combination of either ground beef and pork or ground beef, pork, and veal

1 small onion, chopped

1 garlic clove, minced

½ teaspoon salt

1. Preheat oven to 400°F. Place all ingredients except bread crumbs and pastry in a saucepan. Bring to a boil and cook, uncovered, over medium heat for 20 minutes.

2. Remove from heat and add 3 or 4 spoonfuls of bread crumbs. Let mixture stand for 10 minutes. If the fat is sufficiently absorbed by the bread crumbs, do not add more. If not, add more crumbs in the same manner.

¼ teaspoon celery salt

¼ teaspoon ground cloves (a must for authentic Québécois pie)

½ cup water

¼ to ½ cup bread crumbs

Pastry of your choice for a double-crust 9-inch pie

3. Let mixture cool. Line a 9-inch pie plate with half the pastry and spoon the meat mixture into the plate. Cover with the remaining pastry.

4. Bake until golden brown (follow directions for pie crust you chose) Serve hot.

Note: Cooked tourtière may be frozen for 4 to 5 months and does not need to be thawed before reheating. To reheat, cover your frozen tourtière with foil, place in a medium oven, and bake until a knife inserted into the center is hot when you pull it out.

LOUISE PENNY writes the *New York Times* best-selling Chief Inspector Gamache mysteries. Her novels are set mainly in the fictional village of Three Pines, Quebec. She is a past winner of many coveted awards. *The Long Way Home* is Louise's tenth novel. Louise lives with her husband just outside a small village in Quebec, by the Vermont border.

SCOTT TUROW

Innocent Frittata

In *Innocent*, my sequel to *Presumed Innocent*, the murder victim is allegedly killed by a lethal combination of a drug called phenelzine, an MAO inhibitor, which has a toxic reaction when consumed with sausage, aged cheese, yogurt, and red wine. *Bon appétit!*

YIELD: 1 FRITTATA

1 cup diced dry salami

½ cup canned artichoke hearts, drained and chopped

½ cup cherry tomatoes, chopped

1 4½-ounce can sliced mushrooms, drained

6 eggs

⅓ cup plain yogurt

2 green onions, chopped

1 garlic clove, minced

1 teaspoon dried basil

1 teaspoon onion powder

1 teaspoon salt

Ground black pepper, to taste

½ cup grated mozzarella cheese

½ cup grated aged Parmesan cheese

1. Preheat oven to 425°F. Grease a shallow 2-quart baking dish.

2. Heat skillet over medium heat; cook salami, artichokes, tomatoes, and mushrooms, stirring, until heated through, about 4 minutes. Transfer the mixture to the prepared baking dish.

3. Whisk together eggs, yogurt, green onions, garlic, basil, onion powder, salt, and pepper in a large bowl and then pour over the salami mixture. Sprinkle with both cheeses.

4. Bake until eggs are set and cheese is melted, about 20 minutes.

5. Serve with red wine.

SCOTT TUROW is a writer and attorney. He is the author of ten best-selling works of fiction, including his first novel, *Presumed Innocent* (1987), and the sequel, *Innocent* (2010). His newest novel, *Identical*, was published by Grand Central Publishing in October 2013. He has also written two nonfiction books about his experiences as a lawyer.

LEE CHILD'S RECIPE FOR A
DELICIOUS BEST SELLER

"IT'S LIKE ONE OF THOSE COOKING SHOWS. AT THE BEGINNING of the show, they give the chef a refrigerator of stuff—bean sprouts, honey, pine nuts, chocolate, horseradish, arugula, and—I don't know—beer. And then they say, make something wonderful out of this. The best dish wins.

"So at the beginning of each book, it's as if I'm stocking my story refrigerator. With clues and attitudes, information and ideas, props and personalities. And then, as the story progresses, I know those are the ingredients I'll have to use, beautifully, by the end. I admit sometimes I go back and restock the refrigerator. But often it's the new ideas that come from combinations of those ingredients—the solutions that often reveal themselves just in time—that make the story work."

—Lee Child (see page 171)
as told to Hank Phillippi Ryan (see page 102)

CHRIS PAVONE

Rigatoni a la Bolognese

Before I started writing fiction I was a book editor, and for a while my specialty was cookbooks—I edited thousands upon thousands of recipes, by award-winning chefs and famous TV stars and plain old food writers. I also read countless proposals for cookbooks, as a hobby I perused cookbooks, and of course I cooked a bit. But after all this professional recipe work, my favorite go-to dish has been the same since before I got into the cookbook business. The recipe has evolved over time (I used to include heavy cream, nutmeg, and beef, all now omitted; I dabbled with sausages, sometimes now included), as I have myself. And I'm not claiming this is the *autentico* Bolognese, as indeed neither am I. But it's roughly the same thing I once cooked to try to impress dates, though at this point I haven't been on a first date in eighteen years. Now I use it to try to impress my nine-year-old twins. It still works.

YIELD: 4 SERVINGS

3 tablespoons extra virgin olive oil, divided

1 pound each ground veal and ground pork

Salt and freshly ground black pepper, to taste

1 cup dry white wine

1 tablespoon unsalted butter

1 medium yellow onion, chopped fine

2 carrots, peeled and chopped fine

2 celery stalks, chopped fine

2 tablespoons tomato paste

1 28-ounce can whole San Marzano tomatoes

3 cups chicken broth, divided

2 bay leaves

4 sprigs fresh thyme

4 sprigs fresh oregano

1 pound dried rigatoni

1. Heat 1 tablespoon of the olive oil in a large Dutch oven or other oven-safe heavy-bottomed pot over medium-high heat. When the oil shimmers, add the veal, sprinkle with salt and pepper, and sauté, breaking it up with a wooden spoon until lightly browned, about 5 minutes. Using a slotted spoon, move the meat from the pot to a mixing bowl. Return the pot to the heat. Add a splash of the white wine to the pot, and scrape up any browned bits with the back of a wooden spoon, then pour the contents of the pot into the mixing bowl. Repeat with another tablespoon of oil, the pork, more salt and pepper, and eventually another splash of wine. You'll then have a bowl with a mixture of browned pork and veal and their delicious deglazing juices.

2. Preheat the oven to 300°F.

3. Return the pot to medium heat, add the final tablespoon of oil and the butter, and then the onions. Cook until wilted, about 5 minutes. Add the carrots, celery and salt and pepper to taste, and continue to cook until everything has softened, another 5 minutes. Add the tomato paste and cook, stirring, for 1 minute. Add another splash of white wine to loosen up the mixture, and cook for another minute. Then add the can of tomatoes and 2 cups of the chicken broth, and increase the heat to high. Using a few inches of kitchen twine, tie up the bay leaves, thyme, and oregano, and toss into the pot. When the mixture comes to a boil, pour the contents of the mixing bowl back into the pot and turn off the burner.

4. Transfer the uncovered pot to the oven and cook for 2 hours, stirring occasionally and breaking up the tomatoes with a wooden spoon. If

1 cup whole milk

½ cup freshly grated Parmigiano-Reggiano cheese

1 cup fresh ricotta cheese (optional)

the liquid level gets so low that the solids aren't submerged, add more chicken broth to cover.

5. Bring a large pot of heavily salted water—it should taste like the ocean—to a boil. Add the rigatoni and cook until al dente, according to package directions. *Do not overcook the pasta.* If anything, you want it a tiny bit firmer than ideal for eating; it's going to cook a bit more in the sauce.

6. While the pasta cooks, remove the pot from the oven. If the sauce seems too thin (unlikely, but possible), boil it for a couple minutes over high heat, stirring constantly. Then turn the heat down to medium, add the milk, and simmer, stirring every couple of minutes and making sure the mixture doesn't boil (or else the milk may separate). Fish out the herb bundle and throw it away. This pot contains more sauce than you probably need for the pasta; remove a third of it to a bowl, reserving in case you do want to use it now. If not, pass it at the table or use it another night.

7. Drain the cooked rigatoni, reserving 1 cup of the cooking water. Pour the pasta into the saucepot, and cook for 2 minutes over medium heat, stirring constantly. If the mixture gets too thick or too dry, sprinkle in some of the pasta cooking water, 1 tablespoon at a time. Add more sauce if you want.

8. Remove the pot from the heat and stir in half of the Parmigiano-Reggiano. Gently mix in a few dollops of the ricotta, if using, and serve the rest of both cheeses on the side. Taste for seasoning and serve, which I do directly from the cooking pot, a stained old Le Creuset that my wife bought me eighteen years ago when we'd been dating for just a few months so that I'd be sure to cook this for her for the rest of our lives.

CHRIS PAVONE's *The Expats* was a *New York Times* and international best seller as well as winner of both the Edgar and Anthony awards for best first novel; his second, *The Accident*, is also a *New York Times* best seller. Chris lives in New York City.

GERALD ELIAS

Traditional Umbrian Porchetta

In 1997 and 1998 I enjoyed a sabbatical leave from my position as associate concertmaster of the Utah Symphony. My family and I rented a farmhouse a few miles from the Umbrian hill town of Citta della Pieve. Every Saturday was market day, and I never missed the opportunity to visit the *porchetta* vendor stationed beneath an ancient stone arch, who had been up since before dawn roasting an entire pig of behemoth proportions on a spit. For a modest number of lire, the vendor would sell sliced seasoned meat with morsels of fat, skin, and liver on a fresh hard roll. After I became his favorite customer he agreed to share his recipe. When I returned to the U. S. I experimented with various cuts to try to duplicate the texture and flavor of the original.

In *Devil's Trill*, the first book in my Daniel Jacobus mystery series, there is an episode in which the impecunious family of the seventeenth-century dwarf violin virtuoso, Matteo Cherubino, aka "Il Piccolino," hungrily barters their entertainments for a sampling of porchetta. Though I can't say the vignette was absolutely essential to the story, it was at least a way for me to revisit heaven!

YIELD: 8–10 GENEROUS SERVINGS

1 whole pork picnic shoulder (with bone and skin), approx. 8–10 pounds

About 1 cup olive oil

1 head garlic, cloves separated and peeled but left whole

1 whole fresh fennel bulb

1 to 2 big bunches fresh rosemary

Salt and black pepper, to taste

1 pig's liver, if available

1. Preheat an oven to its lowest setting possible, or preheat a covered gas grill.

2. On a large cutting board with a sharp knife, cut directly toward the shoulder bone of the meat. Butterfly the meat on both sides of the bone, trying to keep the meat about 1 inch thick. (It's better to have it too thick than to cut a piece totally off, but don't worry if you do.)

3. Cover the splayed-out meat with a sheet of plastic wrap and then a kitchen towel. Whack the meat with a mallet until it is all of equal thickness. (This tenderizes it.) Rub olive oil onto the meat.

4. Place some of the garlic cloves, the fennel stalks, some of the rosemary, the salt, a lot of pepper, and the pig liver on the meat. Roll up the roast and tie it tightly with kitchen twine.

5. Finely chop the rest of the garlic. In a bowl, combine it with the olive oil, fennel leaves, the rest of the rosemary, salt, and pepper to make a paste. Generously rub the paste on the outside of the roast.

6. Cook the roast in the oven (with a pan on the rack below to catch the drips) or on the gas grill. On the grill (my preferred method) make sure the meat is *not* above the flame but off to the side, and rotate it 90 degrees every couple of hours. Cook for at least 7 to 8 hours until it falls apart when you cut it. Serve on hard Italian rolls with a little bit of meat, fat, and skin.

GERALD ELIAS, internationally acclaimed violinist, composer, conductor, and author, shines an eerie spotlight on the dark corners of the turbulent classical music world with his award-winning, four-book Daniel Jacobus murder mystery series (St. Martin's Press). His provocative essays and short fiction have also graced many online and prestigious publications.

C. HOPE CLARK

Spicy Crock-Pot Pork

South Carolina screams barbecue, in a Southern genteel manner, of course. We pride ourselves as being the home of all four basic types of barbecue sauce: mustard, vinegar and pepper, light tomato, and heavy tomato, but always served on pork. Other meat can be cooked similarly, but down here only pork is called barbecue. Mustard-based barbecue is our claim to fame, because you find it only in South Carolina, probably derived from German settlers in the 1700s. Vinegar-and-pepper sauce is the second favorite, appreciated more often along the coast, where my Carolina Slade mystery series takes place.

This recipe originated from a need for speed in my house. I dose up the heat depending on who's at the table. Serious barbecue takes careful tending for long hours over a grill, hours I often do not have when in the midst of writing one of Carolina Slade's escapades. As an agricultural investigator, Slade would appreciate a well-cooked pig, in spite of the craziness in *Lowcountry Bribe* involving a murderous, devious, often sleazy hog farmer who nearly stole her job, her family, and, ultimately, her life. While she tired of smelling the pungent aroma of her antagonist's porcine livestock in her chase-and-be-chased experience, she wouldn't be able to deny her Carolina roots and craving for a good piece of pork. I dedicate this recipe to her, a woman on the run who enjoys a good Southern meal.

YIELD: 8 SERVINGS

2 large sweet onions, sliced

2 to 3 pounds boneless pork loin

1 cup hot water

¼ cup sugar, brown or white

3 tablespoons red wine vinegar

2 tablespoons soy sauce

2 tablespoons ketchup

1 teaspoon black pepper

1 teaspoon salt

1 teaspoon diced garlic

1 tablespoon cayenne pepper sauce (Tabasco or similar)

1. Place onions in the bottom of a Crock-Pot or other slow cooker. Place pork on top of onions.

2. In a bowl, combine the rest of the ingredients. Pour over the pork.

3. Cover. Cook on low for 7 hours or on high for 3 to 4 hours.

C. HOPE CLARK pens the award-winning Carolina Slade series, agricultural crime set in gorgeous rural South Carolina, as well as the new Edisto Beach Mystery Series, both via Bell Bridge Books. Hope also founded fundsforwriters.com, one of Writer's Digest's 101 Best Websites for Writers for fourteen years. Her website is chopeclark.com.

LYNDSAY FAYE

Valentine Wilde's Chicken Fricassee

The relationship between brothers Timothy and Valentine Wilde in my book *The Gods of Gotham* and its sequels is a messy one. Their family saga is tragic, their childhoods spent in abject poverty in antebellum Manhattan, and they're about as talented at talking about it as your average plastic grocery bag. Through it all, however, there's a strong thread of affection running through Val's cooking. Despite his struggling with morphine addiction and about every other hedonistic tendency yet recorded, as the series progresses it becomes clearer that his domestic habits were the single gift he could offer his brother when they were orphaned.

In *The Gods of Gotham*, when the brothers' relationship is hostile rather than merely an impossible tangle, Tim urgently mentions finding a job so he won't "have to eat Valentine's goddamned chicken fricassee. My brother can cook as well as he cleans." Since it's a dish that, in Tim's mind, embodies his sibling's annoying culinary skills, I chose it as an example of Val's kitchen prowess as well as the reason he cooks in the first place. It's a big, elegant, sloppy, delicious American home-style dish, a far cry from the fastidious French version. Make it for the people you care about, and you'll make me very pleased.

In developing this recipe, I tried to stay as true as possible to an authentic 1845 model, in which Val would have been using what was immediately to hand during the summer. So feel free to substitute whatever is fresh and available as far as vegetables are concerned. If you can't use homemade chicken stock, farm cream, herbs from your garden, and a heritage red cockerel as I did for the final test of this dish, you know what? You are a perfectly wonderful person, I'd be delighted to know you, and I high-five you for making this dish with whatever ingredients are accessible.

Special thanks must be made to Julia Child, America's Test Kitchen, my husband Gabriel, and especially to Charlotte Campbell Bury, author of *The Lady's Own Cookery Book* published in 1844.

YIELD: 4–6 SERVINGS

1 whole 3-to-4-pound chicken with skin and bones, divided into wings, thighs, legs, and halved breasts

Plenty of salt and freshly cracked black pepper to taste

4 tablespoons (½ stick) butter, divided

2 medium sweet onions, sliced

1. Season the chicken generously with salt and pepper. Melt half of the butter in a large Dutch oven over medium-high heat. After the foaming subsides, arrange chicken in Dutch oven and brown it well, approximately 4 minutes on each side. Once chicken reaches a dark honey brown, remove from Dutch oven and set aside in a bowl to reserve juices.

2. Reduce heat to medium. Add onions and cook until translucent, about 8 minutes, stirring and scraping the bottom of the Dutch oven with a wooden spoon to remove the browned bits.

3. Add the remaining butter, leeks, garlic, and mushrooms and sauté for about 6 minutes. When vegetables have sweated, add brandy and cook, stirring frequently, until liquid has essentially evaporated.

1 large leek, cleaned carefully and sliced into rounds

3 large garlic cloves, minced

10 ounces mushrooms of choice (morels, for instance, were common during this time period, so use whatever you like that's readily available)

¼ cup brandy

2 tablespoons flour

2½ cups chicken stock (homemade is best but not necessary—Val's would have been)

1 large sprig fresh rosemary, broken in half

5 sprigs fresh thyme

3 egg yolks

1 cup high-quality heavy cream (it *does* make a difference if you use good fresh cream)

½ teaspoon freshly grated nutmeg

1 ounce fresh lemon juice

½ cup fresh parsley, chopped

2 teaspoons minced fresh thyme

4. Sprinkle flour over vegetables and stir for about 2 minutes. Pour chicken stock into Dutch oven and incorporate fully into vegetables, being careful to scrape any bits off the bottom or sides with your spoon.

5. Bring mixture to a simmer and return chicken to Dutch oven along with any juices from the bowl. Place rosemary and thyme in the braising liquid—you can tie them together with twine for easier removal if you like. Reduce heat to low and simmer, covered, for 20 to 25 minutes. The chicken is done when an instant-read thermometer reads 160°F for breasts and 175°F for thighs.

6. Meanwhile, whisk egg yolks into heavy cream and set aside on the counter at room temperature.

7. Transfer chicken to a serving dish, and remove and discard rosemary and thyme. Slowly add a ladleful of hot stock to temper the cream and egg mixture, whisking quickly—do not allow the egg to scramble. Repeat this with 2 more ladlefuls of stock. Then pour this mixture into Dutch oven. Stir to combine.

8. Bring mixture in Dutch oven back to a simmer and cook until the sauce thickens to the desired consistency. Add nutmeg, lemon juice, and minced fresh herbs. Season well with salt and pepper to taste. Pour this sauce over the chicken to serve.

Note: Serve the chicken and sauce over pasta, rice, or mashed potatoes, or alternately serve with sliced bread and side dishes of choice.

LYNDSAY FAYE is the internationally best-selling author of the Timothy Wilde trilogy; the first in the series, *The Gods of Gotham*, was nominated for an Edgar Award for Best Novel. She has been recognized by the American Library Association and *Best American Mystery Stories*, and her works have been translated into fourteen languages.

SARA PARETSKY

Chicken Gabriella

Indefatigable Chicago detective V. I. Warshawski was very close to her mother, Gabriella Sestieri, who died when V. I. was 16. Gabriella was a refugee from Umbria living in the shadow of the steel mills on Chicago's Southeast Side. She recreated as much of her childhood home as she could through the olive tree she planted in her front yard, her music, and her cooking. In the books, V. I. often thinks of her mother, often remembers her, especially when drinking from the red Venetian wine glasses that Gabriella brought with her. She also cherishes the recipes of her childhood, and Pollo Gabriella is one that she cooks for special occasions.

YIELD: 4 SERVINGS

Enough olive oil to cover the bottom of a skillet, plus 1 tablespoon

2 garlic cloves, finely chopped

1 fryer chicken, cut into pieces

¼ cup Armagnac

1 cup pinot grigio (or other dry white wine)

6 Calimyrna figs, cut into quarters

1. Coat the bottom of a skillet with olive oil and heat for about 30 seconds. Add garlic and sauté until golden brown, stirring constantly. Remove garlic, and reserve.

2. Add the additional 1 tablespoon olive oil to the skillet. Turn heat to high, quickly add chicken, and sear each piece on both sides.

3. Remove the skillet from the heat. Pour the Armagnac into the skillet, and flame it with a match. (Light the Armagnac the instant you put it in the pan or it will not flame.) Return the pan to the heat.

4. Once the Armagnac has cooked off, add the pinot grigio and simmer the chicken, covered, on low heat until tender, approximately 30 to 45 minutes.

5. Add the figs and sautéed garlic for the last 10 minutes of cooking.

6. Serve with a green salad and a crisp, cold white wine.

Past MWA Grand Master **SARA PARETSKY**, best known for her novels featuring Chicago private eye V. I. Warshawski (most recently *Critical Mass*), is uniquely qualified to write about food: her family's coat of arms is a dinner plate with knife and fork rampant. The motto: "Always Clean Your Plate; Never Skip a Meal."

CHARLES TODD

Chicken Oscar Roulade with Chesapeake Sauce Hollandaise

During World War I, an era we explore in our Ian Rutledge and Bess Crawford novels, there were shortages of many foods, including meats and fresh produce. Because ships were saved for use by the troops, ordinary people depended on their victory gardens and local grocers. During those years, many an hour was spent reminiscing about favorite foods and longing for traditional delicacies and special dishes from farmland devastated by trenches, armies, and tragic loss.

This recipe contains items that were not available to even the finest of restaurants during the "Great War." Of course, we had to add our personal touches and presentation, which are not typical for English cuisine of the era (call it creative license). Today these items are available year round and provide a unique flavor. We also like this dish because the chicken can be prepared in advance, kept cold, and then boiled.

YIELD: 4 SERVINGS

4 6-to-8-ounce boneless skinless chicken breasts

1 package fresh spinach leaves, washed, stemmed, lightly blanched, and laid flat on a paper towel* (do not press the leaves into the paper towel)

1 sweet red bell pepper, cut into straight ⅛-by-⅛-by-3-inch strips and lightly blanched (do not use any of the curved parts of the pepper)

Finely diced fresh parsley (spread on a paper towel to dry)

½ teaspoon Old Bay seasoning

3 6-ounce cans lump crabmeat (or cooked lump crabmeat from the seafood market)

1. Cut 4 pieces of parchment paper 12 inches (the width of the roll) by 10 inches and fold each in half.

2. Trim fat and ligaments from the chicken breasts and place each breast inside a piece of folded parchment paper. Using the side of a meat hammer with small teeth, pound the smooth side of the chicken breasts until they are roughly rectangular pieces with no holes. Yes, George, you can use a regular hammer. Please remember this is not an 8-penny nail, it is dinner.

3. Cut 4 pieces of plastic wrap 12 by 10 inches. Place one piece of chicken (with the flat, smooth side down) on a piece of plastic wrap. Gently rub a light dash of salt and white pepper into each.

4. Cover a piece of chicken with a thin layer of spinach. Line it up exactly so no spinach hangs over the edges and no chicken is visible.

5. Cover the spinach with a thin layer of cooked crabmeat. We all love crab and want lots, but trust me, a thin layer is necessary here! Break up the lumps so the layer is smooth.

6. Place some of the red pepper sticks in a straight line along one of the longer sides of the chicken.

7. Now, starting from the red pepper side, roll the chicken up like a jelly roll, with the pepper in the middle. Be patient! There are do-overs. Assemble one all the way, and then repeat with the others.

1 tablespoon each salt (kosher or sea salt) and ground white pepper (white pepper is twice as strong as black)

Hollandaise sauce (Knorr mix is okay . . . it is best made by hand and kept covered in a place warm to the bare hand. The Joy of Cooking has a nice recipe.) Do not make the sauce until right before service! Be sure to finish with the juice of ½ small lemon and 3 drops Tabasco sauce.

*Blanch means to parboil by plunging a food, usually a vegetable or fruit, into boiling water until either its color has set or it has softened slightly. This takes anywhere from a few seconds to 1 minute, depending on what is being blanched. Then the food is removed to an ice bath to "shock," or stop the cooking process and to set color.

8. Cover the chicken in plastic wrap like a Tootsie Roll; roll it tightly and twist the ends of the plastic wrap so that the ends of the roll are square. Fold the ends of the plastic wrap under the chicken and place on an 8-by-6-inch piece of aluminum foil. Wrap the chicken in the foil and refrigerate. The foil must completely cover the chicken completely and tightly. Congratulations, you have an aluminum hot dog!

9. Fill a 2-quart pot three quarters full of water, bring to a boil (a pinch of salt helps), and place the chicken, foil and all, in the water! Boil for about 20 minutes.

10. Insert a pocket thermometer into one end of the chicken roll until the tip is in the center of the chicken. We want 150°F to 155°F.

11. George is right, chicken should be cooked to 160°F. The meat will continue cook until you unwrap it.

12. Unwrap the chicken. It now holds its shape. Gently slice the roll into rounds, so the spiral shows.

13. Spread hollandaise sauce on a plate and sprinkle with Old Bay (this is for color). Shingle the chicken on the sauce and sprinkle with parsley: With parsley on your hand, flick it on the plate like you are flicking water on your misbehaving child/pet/partner.

14. Serve with small red potatoes roasted in olive oil and tarragon, as well as a bright vegetable. The tiny carrots with the tops on are good.

Note: Always plate things up in the kitchen. Presentation is smell, sight, and then taste. Yes, George, you can have the end pieces!

Under the name **CHARLES TODD**, the team of Caroline and Charles Todd have written twenty-six mysteries, including the Ian Rutledge and Bess Crawford series, and many short stories. A graduate of the Culinary Institute of America, Charles has worked as a chef and director of services at catered events for celebrities, politicians, and former U.S. presidents.

LISA UNGER

Comfort Chicken and Sweet Potatoes

Think Sunday afternoon, snow outside, warm fire inside. Maybe there's a glass of merlot on the counter and something savory roasting in the oven. It's so easy to cook, and so comforting—something that many of us in this busy-addicted world have forgotten. We often think it's easier to drive through, pick up, carry out. But roasting a chicken is one of my very favorite and easiest choices even for a weeknight, in any season. And it really does make any day feel like a leisurely, snowy Sunday—not something I get very often in Florida! You won't believe how easy this is.

YIELD: 4 SERVINGS

1 whole chicken (neck, giblets and whatever other icky bits should be discarded unless you are one of those rare creatures who knows what to do with all that.)

2 tablespoons olive oil, or more to taste

Himalayan sea salt (Really, any kosher salt will do. I'm just being fancy.)

White or black pepper

½ teaspoon each fresh parsley, sage, rosemary, and thyme, or to taste (Hit it, Simon and Garfunkel! Or sometimes oregano, too.)

Red or white onion

5 garlic cloves, minced

Lemon (optional—I usually don't use it. Nothing personal, lemon.)

1 big sweet potato, peeled and cubed

1 cup chicken broth

1. Preheat the oven to 425°F. Wash the chicken in water, dry it, and remove any excess fat around the neck cavity. Rub oil, salt, pepper, and herbs all over the bird, in the cavity and under the skin if possible (don't get cheeky). Stuff the cavity with onion, garlic, and lemon (if you want to use lemon).

2. Put the chicken in a large roasting pan. Arrange the sweet potatoes around the bird. Drizzle oil and seasonings generously on the sweet potatoes. You can put some chicken broth around the sweet potatoes just to keep everything moist and use the broth to baste until the juices and fat start to come off the chicken. Then use those to baste as the bird cooks.

3. Roast the chicken for 15 minutes, and then lower the temperature to 375°F and roast for another 50 minutes to an hour or more (it really depends on your oven). The juices should run clear when the chicken is done, or you can use a meat thermometer to check for doneness. If the potatoes are getting too brown before the chicken is done, cover the pan.

4. Remove the pan from the oven. Put the sweet potatoes in a serving bowl. Let the chicken stand for 20 minutes before carving.

Seriously—you'll feel like Martha. And, of course, what's best about this is that you can use the carcass to make chicken stock and the leftovers for chicken salad the next day. So it's yummy, economical, and time-saving—three meals in one. I know: you're racing out right now to get yourself a chicken! Me, too. I'm starving!

LISA UNGER is an award-winning *New York Times* and internationally best-selling author. Her novels have sold more than 1.7 million copies and have been translated into twenty-six languages.

MARCIA MULLER

Mick's Miracle Chicken

Sharon McCone, the San Francisco–based private detective in my series, is no virtuoso around the kitchen; she's been known to grate her fingers instead of the cheese, confuse flour with sugar (disastrous results), and pour every sticky substance known to humankind on the floor. But she does have one standout recipe, concocted by her nephew, Mick Savage, while he was on the way for a surprise visit to her. As per the following from one of the McCone adventures:

"If he brought and cooked their own dinner, he wouldn't have to sneak out in the middle of the night for a burger. As soon as he spotted the next Safeway, he zipped into its parking lot.

"It wasn't that his aunt couldn't cook, he thought as he drove his Harley—weighted with foodstuff—over to her little house on Church Street. And he thought the kitchen there was terrific. But her schedule of running McCone Investigations, as well as occasionally helping her husband's international security company, RI, frequently made her forget to eat. Tonight she'd be well fed. This recipe that had been developing in his ride on the way back from a client interview in Sonoma would do the trick."

YIELD: 6 SERVINGS, UNLESS MICK SAVAGE HAPPENS TO SHOW UP

2 tablespoons olive oil

8 chicken breast fillets

2 small jars marinated artichoke hearts

2 small jars marinated mushrooms

¼ teaspoon ground white pepper

4 large garlic cloves, or to taste, minced

1 can black olives, whole or chopped

4 ounces fresh shredded or grated Parmesan cheese

1. Preheat oven to 350°F. Heat olive oil in a sauté pan over medium-high heat, and sauté the chicken until browned on both sides. Place in an oven-safe casserole dish.

2. Pour the marinated artichoke hearts over the chicken. You can substitute chicken broth if you don't care for the marinade.

3. Add the mushrooms, white pepper, and garlic to the pan and let the ingredients simmer for 5 to 7 minutes, and then pour over the chicken.

4. Bake for 30 minutes. Top with the Parmesan and bake until the cheese is brown and crusty.

MARCIA MULLER has written many novels and short stories. Her novel *Wolf in the Shadows* won the Anthony Award. She is the recipient of the Private Eye Writers of America Lifetime Achievement Award and the Mystery Writers of America Grand Master Award. She lives in northern California with her husband, mystery writer Bill Pronzini.

BRAD MELTZER

Italian Chicken

All food is memory. It's no different here. Back when I was in high school, this is the meal my girl-friend's mother used to cook for us. It's a chicken dish. Chicken dishes are just that. But somehow, even at eighteen years old, even when I had hair, this was the dish that was better than the rest. When I went off to college, I took this recipe with me. I never made it back then (c'mon, I was in college). Today, though, it still brings back the best memories. And it's still one of my favorites. Read, prepare, eat, enjoy.

YIELD: 4–5 SERVINGS

1 cut-up chicken

Seasoned salt

Black pepper

Garlic salt

1 cup Italian salad dressing

1 8-ounce can mushrooms, sliced or stems and pieces, drained

Grated Parmesan cheese

1. Preheat oven to 350°F. Spray a baking dish with cooking spray.

2. Season chicken to taste with seasoned salt, pepper, and garlic salt.

3. Brush Italian dressing on the skin side of the chicken and place, skin side down, in prepared baking dish. Brush remaining dressing on chicken to coat.

4. Bake chicken for 30 minutes. Remove from oven and turn chicken so the skin side is up.

5. Put mushrooms around chicken. Sprinkle cheese on top of chicken. Bake for another 30 to 40 minutes, until chicken is nicely browned.

BRAD MELTZER is the #1 *New York Times* best-selling author of *The Inner Circle*, *The Book of Fate*, and seven other best-selling thrillers. He is also one of the only authors to ever have books on the best seller lists for fiction, nonfiction, advice, children's books, and even comic books. His website is bradmeltzer.com.

KARNA SMALL BODMAN

International Chicken and Pilaf

I served this family recipe to members of the delegation visiting Washington, D.C., with the president of Egypt (I had a friend in the group). I remember talking about international challenges as well as friendship—and now I use both themes in my novels. You might enjoy sharing this main dish with friends and "sources" for your next mystery or thriller.

YIELD: 8 SERVINGS

CHICKEN

2 tablespoons butter

1 medium onion, chopped

8 large chicken pieces (thighs and breasts)

1 cup chopped celery

1 cup chopped fresh parsley (use scissors to chop)

1 cup dry white wine

1 cup chicken broth

¼ cup heavy cream

PILAF

1 tablespoon butter

2 "handfuls" angel hair pasta

1 cup Uncle Ben's regular rice

3 cups chicken broth, heated

1. For the chicken: Melt butter in a large skillet. Add onions and cook until golden. Then add chicken pieces and brown them. Add celery, parsley, wine, and broth. Cover and simmer for one hour.

2. While the chicken is cooking, make the pilaf: Melt butter in a 2-quart saucepan. Break pasta into shorter pieces and add to pan. Add rice and stir together. When both rice and pasta are golden, add warmed chicken broth. Cover and simmer for 30 minutes or less (check it periodically).

3. When chicken is done, remove it to a platter. Add cream to pan, heat to reduce sauce, and then pour sauce over chicken. Serve chicken over the pilaf.

KARNA SMALL BODMAN, author of four published novels (that have hit "#1 in Thrillers" on Amazon), served for six years in the White House. Her last post was senior director of the National Security Council. Her latest international thriller, *Castle Bravo*, won several awards and is available in print, e-book, and audio formats on karnabodman.com.

L. J. SELLERS

Chicken Enchiladas

As a busy crime fiction author—who's released twelve books in the last six years—I barely have time to cook. But whenever my extended family gets together, they always want me to make my chicken enchiladas. And who can say no to family? My sons have almost come to blows over the last serving. And this delicious casserole dish is guaranteed to make you popular at potlucks.

YIELD: ABOUT 10

1 pint light sour cream

1 can cream of chicken soup

1 small can diced green chilies

2 cups grated sharp cheddar cheese

Salt and black pepper, to taste

3 large chicken breasts, cooked and diced

10 or so tortillas (flour or white corn)

1. Preheat oven to 350°F. Lightly grease or spray an oven dish or roasting pan.

2. Combine all ingredients except chicken and tortillas.

3. Roll up a portion of chicken in each tortilla with 1 tablespoon of sauce mixture. Lay rolled-up tortillas side by side in the prepared pan.

4. When pan is full, cover enchiladas with the rest of the sauce and bake for about 25 minutes.

5. Help yourself to a large portion because there won't be any leftovers.

L. J. SELLERS writes the best-selling Detective Jackson mysteries—a two-time Readers Favorite winner—as well as the Agent Dallas series and stand-alone thrillers. L. J., an award-winning journalist, resides in Eugene, Oregon. When not plotting murders, she enjoys stand-up comedy, cycling, and social networking. She has also been known to jump out of airplanes.

HANK PHILLIPPI RYAN

Worth-the-Effort Turkey Tetrazzini

There's no such thing as a holiday for a reporter, so the last time Jane Ryland, the main character in my series of stand-alone thrillers, sat down to a fabulous holiday dinner is—well, never. I know the feeling. As a reporter for the last forty years, I'm often working on Thanksgiving, so all I get are the leftovers. However, making something out of nothing is the hallmark of a good reporter—as well as a good storyteller. And in this case, it's especially wonderful if the "nothing" includes wine and fresh mushrooms. And leftovers.

First, get the leftovers from a roast turkey. Then, read the recipe before you start because its success depends on doing several things at the same time—and having the ingredients prepped and the utensils ready to go. It sounds a little more complicated than it is. The first time I made it I burst out laughing—it looked like I had used every pan I owned. Now I've made it so often I don't even need the recipe!

You can use more or less pasta and mushrooms and turkey—it doesn't really matter. An added bonus—your kitchen will smell fantastic while this is cooking. This reheats beautifully and is delicious and decadent. We look forward to this just as much as our holiday turkey.

YIELD: 6–8 SERVINGS

1 pound mushrooms

4½ tablespoons butter, divided

1 garlic clove, or more to taste, chopped

¼ to ½ pound spaghetti or macaroni

3 tablespoons flour

2 cups chicken broth

1 cup heated whipping cream (fat-free half-and-half will also work)

3 tablespoons dry white wine

Salt and black pepper

2 to 3 cups shredded cooked turkey

Grated Parmesan cheese

1. Preheat the oven to 375°F and bring a large pot of water to boil.

2. Sauté the mushrooms in 1½ tablespoons of the butter and garlic. Keep warm. When the water comes to a rolling boil, add the pasta.

3. Melt the remaining 3 tablespoons butter in another saucepan. Sprinkle the butter with the flour. Stir to make a paste, and then add the chicken broth. Cook until the mixture thickens, about 15 minutes.

4. Remove the butter mixture from heat and stir in the heated cream, wine, salt, and pepper.

5. When the pasta is finished, drain it, put it back in the pan and mix in the sautéed mushrooms. Add one-half of the butter-cream sauce.

6. Place the turkey in a bowl and add the other half of the sauce.

7. Transfer the pasta mixture to a greased baking dish. Make a hole in the center, and pour in the turkey-sauce mixture. Sprinkle the top with the Parmesan cheese.

8. Bake until lightly browned and cooked through, about 20 minutes.

HANK PHILLIPPI RYAN is an on-air investigative reporter for Boston's NBC affiliate, winning thirty-two Emmys and dozens of other honors. A best-selling author of six mysteries, Ryan has won three Agathas and the Anthony, Macavity, and Mary Higgins Clark awards. A founder of MWA University and the 2013 president of Sisters in Crime, her newest book is *Truth Be Told*.

CAROLYN HART

Simple Salmon

One of the joys of writing is creating characters you'd like to know. In *Death on Demand*, the first in my series, Annie Laurance is running a mystery bookstore on a South Carolina sea island when her boyfriend, Max, arrives. Who was Max? Hey, it's fiction, so why not make him the perfect guy: tall, blond, handsome, rich, and a great cook. Despite their different backgrounds (he grew up rich, she grew up poor; he sees life as a romp, she is strongly imbued with a puritan work ethic), Max wins her heart. In *Dead, White and Blue*, their twenty-third adventure, Annie and Max are still young and happy on their sea island and Max fixes his favorite salmon dish as they wonder how a woman could disappear into the pines and never be seen again.

YIELD: VARIABLE, WITH BELOW ADJUSTMENTS

5- or 6-ounce fresh salmon fillets (1 fillet per person)

Olive oil

3 tablespoons lemon juice per fillet

Black pepper

TARTAR SAUCE

4 tablespoons mayonnaise (I prefer Hellmann's)

1½ tablespoons sweet pickle relish

Dash mustard

¼ cup chopped onions (optional)

1. Preheat oven to 350°F. Line a cooking tray or pan with foil and moisten foil with olive oil.

2. Place salmon skin side down on foil. Pour lemon juice over each fillet and sprinkle lightly with pepper.

3. Tent a piece of foil over pan to enclose fillets. (This will make salmon succulent.)

4. Bake for 15 minutes.

5. To make Max's Homemade Tartar Sauce, combine all tartar sauce ingredients and chill.

Note: This is delicious when served with rice pilaf. To make the pilaf: Sauté 1 small chopped onion in 2 tablespoons butter. Add rice and 1 cup beef bouillon per serving of rice and cook for 20 minutes, or until rice is done.

CAROLYN HART, a 2014 MWA Grand Master, is the author of fifty-three novels of mystery and suspense. Her latest are *Cliff's Edge*, suspense in first-century Rome; *Ghost Wanted*, fifth in the Bailey Ruth series; and *Don't Go Home*, twenty-fifth in the Death on Demand series.

KIM FAY

Caramelized Clay Pot Fish

While living in Vietnam for four years, I fell in love with the cultures and cuisine of the region. It was this love that inspired me to write *The Map of Lost Memories* and to spend an additional three years researching *Communion*—and by researching, I mean eating to my heart's content.

There are very few Vietnamese dishes I dislike, and many on my list of favorites. In the latter category, Caramelized Clay Pot Fish is at the top. This dish is most popular in the south of the country, where I lived and sampled it often, but it wasn't until I took a five-week journey to cook with chefs throughout the country that I truly understood how nuanced it is.

In most recipes the base ingredients are the same. It is the way they are combined that creates individuality. For my version, I tested and tasted to achieve the characteristic that makes Vietnamese food a standout for me: balance. With the right combination of sugar, salt (in the fish sauce), chili, and ginger, the flavor of Caramelized Clay Pot Fish is unforgettable. And on a chilly day, this dish is comfort food at its best. Because of this it will be one of dishes featured in my novel in progress, *To Feed Such Hunger*, when the main character, a culinary anthropologist, needs solace after her best friend is murdered in 1960s Vietnam.

YIELD: 2 SERVINGS

FISH

1 pound firm white fish such as halibut, cut into 1-inch chunks (chicken, pork, or shrimp can also be used)

1½ tablespoons fish sauce (Try to buy Vietnamese fish sauce and avoid any brand that has ingredients other than anchovies and salt. My top choice is Red Boat.)

Up to 1½ tablespoons peanut oil

SAUCE

2 tablespoons peanut oil

6 tablespoons sugar

4 tablespoons minced shallots

1. Prepare the fish: Marinate the fish in the fish sauce and oil for half an hour at room temperature.

2. While the fish marinates, prepare the sauce. Heat oil in a heavy-bottom saucepan. Add the sugar and stir until the sugar dissolves. The mixture may seem too dry at first, or the sugar may crystallize a bit. Be patient, and keep stirring. Make sure the heat is high enough. Eventually, the sugar will dissolve.

3. Add the shallots, garlic, and ginger.

4. Add coconut juice. (Make sure it's warm before you add it. If not, the cold liquid hitting the hot oil/sugar will cause an instant case of hard candy. If this happens, just keep stirring until the "candy" dissolves.)

5. Stir in the chilies and then the fish sauce, and add the black pepper.

6. Bring the sauce to a boil and then lower to a simmer.

7. Once the fish has marinated and the sauce has been prepared, warm your clay pot with a cup or so of hot water. This will keep it from cracking as it heats up on the stove. This is especially important for a new pot. (If you do not have a clay pot, you can substitute a heavy-bottom 2-quart saucepan.)

2 garlic cloves, minced

2 1-inch chunks ginger, peeled

1 cup coconut juice (aka coconut water, not coconut milk), warmed

2 whole red Thai chilies

1 tablespoon fish sauce

Pinch ground black pepper

8. Discard the water from pot and add the fish. Pour the remainder of the marinade over the fish.

9. Put the clay pot with fish in it on a burner on low. Don't brown the fish, but simply warm it up a bit.

10. Add sauce to the clay pot and simmer, covered, for 20 minutes.

11. Remove chilies and ginger before serving. Serve over rice.

KIM FAY is the author of *The Map of Lost Memories*, an Edgar Award finalist for Best First Novel by an American Author. She has also written the food memoir *Communion: A Culinary Journey through Vietnam*, winner of the Gourmand World Cookbook Award for Best Asian Cuisine Book in the U.S.

KATHY REICHS

Shrimp Scampi

I live in Charlotte, North Carolina, and own a beach home on a barrier island outside Charleston, South Carolina. Like my character, Temperance Brennan, I constantly shift between the two locations. Whether in the piedmont or the low country, one thing remains constant. My family and I eat a lot of seafood. Especially shrimp.

Shrimp is plentiful year round in my neck of the woods. And versatile. I am always scouting new ways to prepare it. At times, I feel like Forrest Gump's pal, Bubba. You can barbecue it, boil it, broil it, bake it, sauté it, deep-fry, pan-fry, or stir-fry it. There's shrimp kabobs, shrimp creole, shrimp gumbo, pineapple shrimp, lemon shrimp, coconut shrimp, pepper shrimp, shrimp soup, shrimp stew, shrimp salad, shrimp and potatoes, shrimp burger, shrimp sandwich . . . You get the idea.

Point of information: Though I love eating, I hold no fondness for chopping and slicing and dicing. Quick and easy, that's my kind of cooking.

This recipe for shrimp scampi has been one of my favorites for decades. The only labor intensive part is peeling the little crustaceans. Even that can be skipped, if you prefer.

YIELD: 4 SERVINGS

2 pounds fresh shrimp (the bigger the better)

2 teaspoons chopped fresh garlic (feel free to ramp it up)

Crushed red pepper flakes, to taste (anywhere from $1/8$ teaspoon on up)

$1/2$ teaspoon dried crushed oregano (or go with fresh if you have it)

2 tablespoons fine fresh bread crumbs

$1/2$ cup extra virgin olive oil

Salt and freshly ground black pepper, to taste

1. Set the broiler to high.

2. Peel and devein the shrimp, and either leave the tails attached or remove them (I leave them on). Rinse and pat dry.

3. Mix the remaining ingredients and toss with the shrimp to coat evenly.

4. Line a baking dish or cookie sheet with foil and arrange the shrimp on it in one layer.

5. Place the shrimp 3 to 4 inches under the broiler for 5 to 6 minutes. It is not necessary to turn them as they cook.

6. Baste the shrimp and serve hot over rice.

KATHY REICHS's first novel *Déjà Dead* was an international sensation. Her seventeen other Temperance Brennan novels include *Fatal Voyage*, *Monday Mourning*, *Devil Bones*, *Spider Bones*, *Bones of the Lost*, and *Bones Never Lie*. She is a producer of the TV series *Bones* and coauthor of the young adult Virals books.

BARBARA ROSS

Lobster-Pesto Risotto

The family in my Maine Clambake Mystery series offers their guests a scenic harbor cruise and an authentic clambake on a private island during Maine's short tourist season. You'd think serving 1,200 pounds of lobster to 400 tourists a day might turn someone off the fresh, local ingredient, but owner and manager Julia Snowden has discussed this thoroughly with the local family that runs the ice cream parlor, and her conclusion is, "If you love something, you love *it*."

YIELD: 6–8 SERVINGS

5 cups seafood stock

1 tablespoon olive oil

1 onion, chopped

2 cups arborio rice

1 cup dry white wine

1 pound cooked lobster meat, chopped

4 tablespoons pesto, plus extra for serving

2 tablespoons unsalted butter

Salt and pepper, to taste

Parmesan cheese for serving

1. Heat seafood stock in saucepan; do not boil.

2. In another saucepan, heat oil over medium heat. Add onion and sauté for 5 minutes.

3. Add rice to oil and stir to coat the grains. Cook for 2 to 3 minutes.

4. Add wine to oil and rice and stir until it has been absorbed.

5. Begin adding the warmed seafood stock by the ladleful, stirring after each ladleful until it is absorbed and rice is creamy. This process should take 15 to 20 minutes.

6. Stir in lobster, the 4 tablespoons of pesto, and butter, and season with salt and pepper. Cook for 2 minutes longer.

7. Plate and serve with a dollop of pesto. Offer Parmesan cheese for those who would like it.

BARBARA ROSS writes the Maine Clambake Mysteries. The latest is *Boiled Over*. The first, *Clammed Up*, was nominated for the Agatha Award for Best Novel and the *RT Book Reviews* Reviewers' Choice Best Book Award for Amateur Sleuth and was a finalist for the Maine Literary Award for Crime Fiction.

LINDA FAIRSTEIN

Angel Hair Pasta with Scallops and Shallots

At the end of a long writing day on Martha's Vineyard, there is nothing more delicious than this recipe of my mother's. If you are lucky enough to find those tiny, sweet Nantucket Bay scallops in your local market (like my series character Alex "Coop" Cooper and I do), they're the ones to use. If not, be sure to cut larger scallops into small bites.

YIELD: 4 SERVINGS	
1 box angel hair pasta	1. Cook the pasta according to the package directions. Meanwhile, in a frying pan, sauté the shallots in olive oil.
3 shallots, chopped	
A splash of olive oil	2. When the shallots began to brown, add the scallops, stirring briskly until they're opaque. (Stay on it! They cook quickly and get way too chewy if overdone.)
1 pound scallops	
A few sprigs of chopped parsley	3. As the scallops cook, add the parsley to the pan, along with the lemon juice and 3 tablespoons of water from the cooking pasta.
2 tablespoons lemon juice	
Parmesan cheese to taste	4. The pasta should be al dente as soon as the scallops are done. Drain in a colander.
	5. Transfer the pasta to a bowl, add the scallops and shallots, and sprinkle lightly with the cheese.
	6. Serve with garlic bread, open a delicious bottle of white wine, and savor the dish.

LINDA FAIRSTEIN, former sex crimes prosecutor in the Manhattan DA's office and author of the best-selling legal thrillers featuring Alex Cooper, has been a member of the MWA for more than two decades. Her latest New York Times best seller is 2014's *Terminal City*.

CAROLE BUGGÉ

Tuna a la Varenka

A few years ago, I was living in a cabin in the woods in Woodstock (yes, that Woodstock) working on *Silent Screams*, the first of my Lee Campbell thrillers. I had never written about serial killers before, and it was a little nerve-wracking to be in a cabin equipped with only a hook and eye lock a clever five-year old could pry open. (Such is life in Byrdcliffe Arts Colony, which is long on rustic charm but short on basic upkeep.) I had no car at the time, only my trusty bicycle that had taken me over 200 miles on the rail trail from Cumberland, Maryland, to Georgetown in Washington, D.C.

One July afternoon I jumped on my bicycle and pedaled down to Sunfrost, my local green grocer, to see what they had in the way of fish. My friend Matt (the owner) said some fresh tuna had just come in, so I bought it. I prepared this dish while the acorns cascaded down on my roof and my striped cat sat smiling in the sunlight streaming in through white lace curtains. (Varenka was the name of my cabin, by the way—all the cabins in Byrdcliffe have charmingly whimsical names.)

YIELD: 2 SERVINGS

1 pound tuna steaks (or whatever fish you like)

⅓ cup flour

1 cup diced peppers

1 cup diced onion

2 tablespoons sesame oil

1 teaspoon fresh garlic

1 teaspoon fresh ginger

1 cup mango

Red pepper flakes

Black pepper

¼ teaspoon soy sauce

2 tablespoons corn syrup

2 tablespoons honey

2 tablespoons cream sherry

2 tablespoons ground dried orange peel

Dash wasabi powder

1. Roll fish fillets in flour until covered on both sides.

2. Sauté fish, peppers, and onions in sesame oil in a large iron skillet.

3. Add other ingredients and simmer for approximately 10 minutes, until fish is tender and cooked through.

CAROLE BUGGÉ (aka C. E. Lawrence) has nine published novels, award-winning plays, musicals, poetry, and short fiction. Her work has appeared in two MWA anthologies, and *Silent Stalker* is the latest Lee Campbell thriller. She has been featured in *China Grove Literary Magazine*. Visit her online at celawrence.com.

LAURA JOH ROWLAND

Crab Cakes

I'm a rare phenomenon—a Chinese-Korean American who writes a historical mystery series set in Japan, is bad at math, and detests onions. I write about Japan because I saw too many samurai movies when I was in college. I don't know why the math or the onions. Maybe it's because I started school at age four, and my brain wasn't developed enough to process numbers and I never caught up. Maybe I smelled too many onions when my grandmother was chopping them to make kimchi. Life has sometimes been difficult because of my quirks, and not only while I was struggling to learn calculus. I love crab cakes, but I can never eat them in restaurants because they're always chock full of onions. So I use my own, onion-free recipe for crab cakes. I substitute fresh parsley and dill. I have served these to many people, who loved them and never complained about the missing onions.

YIELD: 12 CRAB CAKES

1 pound fresh lump crabmeat

2 tablespoons chopped fresh parsley

2 tablespoons chopped fresh dill

1 tablespoon mayonnaise

1 garlic clove, minced

1 large egg, lightly beaten

Juice of $1/2$ lemon

$1/8$ teaspoon ground cayenne pepper

$1/4$ cup panko bread crumbs

6 tablespoons olive oil, divided

1. Mix together all the ingredients except the olive oil.

2. Form into patties approximately $1/2$ inches thick and 2 inches in diameter.

3. Warm 3 tablespoons olive oil in a large skillet over medium-high heat. Add half the patties. Fry until golden, 2 to 3 minutes on each side.

4. Repeat with the remaining oil and patties.

LAURA JOH ROWLAND is the author of a mystery series set in medieval Japan featuring samurai detective Sano Ichiro. Her work has been published in fourteen countries and won the RT Award for Best Historical Mystery. Her latest book is *The Iris Fan*. Laura lives in New York City.

CHAPTER FIVE

Ladies and gentlemen of the jury, you have seen all of the evidence. And you understand the charge: My client has been wrongly accused of too many side dishes.

MODEL 1

S. J. ROZAN

Rancho Obsesso Lavender Beets

For the past twenty years, I've rented a summer house with the same group of friends: a musician, an architecture critic, a college professor, an architect, and me, the writer. Everyone in the house is a little, er, focused on their work. One morning years ago, a guest wandered downstairs after a good night's sleep, ready for breakfast, a book in the hammock, maybe the beach, only to find us each settled in a different nook with our laptops. The phone rang; the guest picked it up and said, "Rancho Obsesso." Well, okay, we work hard, but we cook harder. This is one of our go-to recipes.

YIELD: 4–6 SERVINGS

6 cups beets cut into
1-inch chunks

2 cups carrots cut into
1-inch chunks

¼ to ½ cup olive oil

¼ cup fresh culinary
lavender, chopped

Coarse (kosher) salt

1. Preheat oven to 400°F.

2. Combine beets, carrots, olive oil, and lavender in a bowl. Mix until vegetables are thoroughly coated (use as much olive oil as necessary).

3. Spread vegetables in a roasting pan and sprinkle with salt; place in oven.

4. Check every 10 minutes, stirring when you check. When vegetables are fork-tender and beginning to brown, they're done.

S. J. ROZAN is the author of the Lydia Chin/Bill Smith series and half of the Sam Cabot team behind the Novels of Secrets series. She has won most of crime fiction's top awards, including the Edgar, Anthony, and Shamus. Her latest book is Sam Cabot's *Skin of the Wolf*.

PRETTY POISONS
RIGHT IN YOUR GARDEN

AS LEGENDARY MYSTERY AUTHOR P. D. JAMES HAS POINTED OUT, POISONS WERE a popular means of murder for many centuries, starting with man's earliest history, and especially favored by the Borgia family (which included two popes) during the Italian Renaissance. Though it's well known that some women have used poison to rid themselves of unwanted or abusive husbands, pharmacist and toxicologist Luci Hansson Zahray believes the notion that poison is a "woman's crime" is a misconception. "The famous poisoners are all male," she stresses.

Poison has plenty of advantages as a murder weapon. As Zahray points out, "it's silent and invisible, usually leaves no sign of trauma, allows a weaker person to easily overcome a physically or mentally stronger one, and is buried with the victim." An extra bonus for the squeamish murderer: you don't have to be physically present to kill. "Ninety percent of poisonings are fatal," says Zahray, an MWA member who is often called "The Poison Lady" because of her expertise. "Poisons can fairly easily be made to look like an accident or suicide, or it's wrongly assumed that the victim died of disease or natural causes."

What about toxicology screens? Aren't they supposed to spot poison in the system? Unfortunately they typically test for just a small range of substances, such as alcohol, narcotics, sedatives, marijuana, cocaine, amphetamines, acetaminophen, and aspirin. The police would have to suspect a particular poison to have the medical examiner run a screen for it.

Zahray believes that poisonings are far more common than we realize. "All one has to do is look at the number of poisonings that are first documented only after the exhumation of the deceased in order to raise the logical question, 'If we missed this one, how many more have been missed?'" She reveals that some of the most dangerous poisons are right in our gardens and can be added to food with no one being the wiser. A brilliant idea if you're plotting the murder of, er, that character in the mystery you're writing.

According to Zahray, the seeds of the toxic datura plant (also known as devil's trumpet) look a bit like red pepper flakes when dried and could be sprinkled in a dish. The seeds (or "beans") of the castor oil plant, which contain the poisonous substance ricin, resemble pinto beans and can be mixed in a stew. (Ricin is considered second only to botulism toxin as the most poisonous compound known to man.) Their shells soften with cooking, and it would only take eight to make someone very ill.

You could also make a deadly afternoon tea by soaking the flowers or leaves of foxgloves, lilies of the valley, and oleanders. They all contain toxic cardiac glycosides.

Most devious of all? Poisoning someone with a several of these substances at the same time, says Zahray. It would create a crazy mix of symptoms, totally confusing a local medical examiner.

—Kate White

HALLIE EPHRON

Simplest Ever Potato Pancakes

These homemade potato pancakes are one of those labor-intensive but super easy and spectacularly delicious treats that cannot be matched by anything store-bought or ordered in a restaurant. When I've had a hard day writing, grating and cooking them is the ultimate mind cleanser. Eating them is the perfect reward.

My advice: do not attempt to cook anything else at the same time. Prepare them. Fry them in batches. Eat them hot as they come out of the pan (after a quick rest to drain on paper towel). If you insist on being an overachiever and serving these with a meal, they can be drained and then put in a warm oven on a cookie rack (so the air circulating all around keeps them crisp).

Caution: Once you start preparing, don't stop until all the potatoes are cooked. Grated potatoes left to stand will turn dark and yucky looking.

YIELD: 4 SERVINGS

2 large unpeeled potatoes (russets work well)

1 egg

Flour

Cooking oil (vegetable or peanut oil; not olive oil) for frying

1. Hand-grate the potatoes using the large holes on the grater (the results will be much crisper and more satisfying if you use a hand grater, which produces thinner pieces than a food processor).

2. Dump the grated potatoes into a clean dish towel; wring out as much liquid as you can over the sink. Squeeze, and squeeze again!

3. Dump the wrung-out potatoes into a mixing bowl; add the egg and a scant handful of flour. Mix.

4. Form mixture into 1-tablespoon pancakes.

5. Heat oil in a frying pan until a bit of potato sizzles when it hits the oil.

6. Ladle pancakes into the hot oil. Don't crowd the pan. Flatten and cook until golden brown and crisp on one side, then turn and cook until golden brown and crisp on the other.

7. Drain cooked potato pancakes on paper towel. If they don't get scarfed up immediately, put them on a cookie rack in a warm (200°F) oven until ready to serve.

8. Cook batches until all are cooked.

9. Serve with salt and, if you like, applesauce or sour cream.

HALLIE EPHRON is an award-winning book reviewer and best-selling author of nine suspense novels including *Never Tell a Lie* and *There Was an Old Woman*. Her latest novel is *Night Night, Sleep Tight*.

EDITH MAXWELL
Local Leek Tart

Geek turned organic farmer Cam Flaherty grows produce for members of the Locavore Club, a quirky group of local foods enthusiasts. As Cam finishes the fall harvest, she has no idea that a toxic threat to her quiet life as a farmer festers under society's topsoil. In *'Til Dirt Do Us Part,* one of the guests at her farm-to-table dinner is found dead in a pigsty the next day.

Leeks and herbs are part of the weekly share at Cam's farm. When she's not out weeding or sleuthing, she likes to combine them with a neighboring farm's goat cheese to make this tasty leek tart.

YIELD: 8–10 SERVINGS

3 tablespoons olive oil, divided

3 pounds cleaned leeks (preferably local), white parts and 1 inch of pale green parts, thinly sliced

2 teaspoons fresh thyme leaves

1/2 cup chicken stock (or vegetable stock)

1 teaspoon salt, divided

3/4 teaspoon freshly ground pepper, divided

1/3 cup crème fraîche

3 ounces soft herbed goat cheese, preferably local, crumbled

1/2 pound mushrooms, preferably local, brushed clean and coarsely chopped

All-purpose flour for dusting

1 sheet puff pastry, thawed if frozen

1. In a sauté pan over medium-high heat, warm 2 tablespoons of the oil. Add the leeks and sauté until translucent, 4 to 5 minutes. Add the thyme, stock, 1/2 teaspoon of the salt, and 1/2 teaspoon of the pepper. Reduce the heat to low, cover, and simmer until the leeks are nearly tender, about 15 minutes. Uncover and cook, stirring occasionally and being careful not to let the leeks brown, until almost all the liquid has evaporated, about 15 minutes more.

2. Transfer the leeks to a bowl. Stir in the crème fraîche and goat cheese until well mixed.

3. In another pan over medium-high heat, warm the remaining 1 tablespoon oil. Add the mushrooms and the remaining 1/2 teaspoon salt and 1/4 teaspoon pepper. Sauté until the mushrooms are soft and have released their juices, 3 to 4 minutes.

4. Preheat oven to 400°F. Line a large rimmed baking sheet with parchment paper.

5. On a floured work surface, roll out the puff pastry to a 10-by-12-inch rectangle about 1/8 inch thick. Transfer the dough to the prepared baking sheet. Spread the leek mixture to within 1 inch of the edge of the dough, and fold the edges of the dough over the filling to make a free-form tart.

6. Bake until the crust puffs and both the crust and the leeks are golden, about 15 minutes. Scatter the mushrooms over the leeks and bake for 5 minutes more.

7. Let the tart stand for 5 to 10 minutes. Cut into squares and serve warm.

EDITH MAXWELL's latest Local Foods Mystery is *'Til Dirt Do Us Part* (Kensington Publishing). She also writes the Lauren Rousseau mysteries as Tace Baker (Barking Rain Press), the historical Carriagetown Mysteries, and award-winning short crime fiction. A mother, traveler, and technical writer, Edith blogs every weekday from Massachusetts at wickedcozyauthors.com.

DARYL WOOD GERBER AKA AVERY AAMES

Cheddar-Monterey Jack Cheese Sauce with Broccoli

Because I write the Cookbook Nook Mysteries as well as the Cheese Shop Mysteries, I often like to blend the two worlds when it comes to cooking. In the Cookbook Nook series, Jenna Hart, a former ad exec, returns home to Crystal Cove, California, to help her aunt open a culinary bookshop and café. Jenna is an avid reader and a foodie, but she is not a cook. In the Cheese Shop series, Charlotte Bessette, the owner of a gourmet cheese shop in the quaint fictional town of Providence, Ohio, is a fabulous cook and, of course, she adores cheese. This recipe is the perfect match for both ladies. The flavor is divine, and there aren't so many ingredients that Jenna might mess it up!

YIELD: 8 SERVINGS

½ cup (1 stick) butter

½ cup cornstarch

2 teaspoons salt, divided

½ teaspoon ground white or black pepper

1 teaspoon Worcestershire sauce

¼ cup dry white wine

4 cups milk (may be 2%)

1 cup (4 ounces) shredded cheddar cheese

1 cup (4 ounces) Monterey Jack or Havarti cheese

2 heads broccoli

Dash paprika for garnish, if desired

1. In a saucepan over medium heat, melt the butter. Stir in the cornstarch, 1 teaspoon of the salt, and pepper.

2. Gradually add the Worcestershire sauce, wine, and milk and stir.

3. Bring the mixture to a boil and cook for about 2 minutes, stirring constantly, until the mixture is thickened.

4. Lower the heat and add the cheeses. Stir until the cheeses are melted.

5. And, now, to make perfect broccoli: Cut each head of broccoli into quarters, removing the hard end. Bring 1 inch of water in a large pot to a boil. Add the remaining 1 teaspoon salt. Add the broccoli, cover, and boil for 4 minutes. Remove from heat; pour off the water. Cover the pot and let the broccoli steam for 4 more minutes. Remove the lid and rinse the broccoli with cold water to stop the cooking process. Pour off the cold water.

6. Set broccoli quarters on plates, and pour the cheese sauce over them. Sprinkle with paprika, if desired. Serve warm.

Note: This recipe makes a large portion of sauce. You can refrigerate any remaining sauce and reheat it in the microwave. It is fabulous poured over baked potatoes, other veggies, and pasta.

DARYL WOOD GERBER writes the nationally best-selling Cookbook Nook Mystery series. As Avery Aames, she pens the nationally best-selling Cheese Shop Mystery series. Her latest titles are *Stirring the Plot* and *As Gouda as Dead*. Fun tidbit: as an actress, Daryl appeared in *Murder, She Wrote* and more. Visit Daryl or Avery at darylwoodgerber.com.

DIANA CHAMBERS

Tahdig (Traditional Crusty Persian Rice)

In my second Nick Daley novel, *The Company She Keeps*, we meet his new agent, Evelyn Walker. Bruised by her CIA experiences, "E" leaves the Company to begin life anew in Paris. There she falls in love with a romantic Iranian and moves with him to Tehran in the early 1990s. Before being swept up by political intrigue, she learns the art of making *tahdig*, a beloved Persian recipe, from Karim's old nanny.

YIELD: ENOUGH FOR 4–8 PEOPLE, WHO MAY VIE OVER THE CRISPY TOP

2½ cups basmati rice

2 teaspoons salt (or to taste), divided

1 thread saffron

2 cups plain yogurt

4 tablespoons unsalted butter

1. Rinse rice in colander under cold running water until the water runs clear (5 to 10 times). Remove any impurities. Drain.

2. Place rice and 1 teaspoon of the salt in a saucepan, and then cover with 4 cups of water (by tradition, "one thumb-length of water"). Bring to a boil and simmer for about 5 minutes. Rice will be al dente, not mushy.

3. Drain the rice and reserve the liquid. Soften saffron in "half a small tea glass" of reserved liquid for 5 minutes.

4. Place yogurt in a bowl, and then add saffron water, rice, and the remaining 1 teaspoon salt. Stir just enough to coat the rice.

5. Melt butter in a deep skillet, then add the rice and form it into a mound. Poke 7 holes in the mounded rice and cover the pan. Cook on high heat for 10 minutes, periodically rotating the pan on the burner to cook it evenly.

6. Reduce the heat to low, and cook for 30 to 60 minutes, watching for the water to absorb and adding reserved liquid little by little until done.

7. Invert the rice onto a plate, revealing the golden brown crust, fragrant and still sizzling.

DIANA CHAMBERS was born with a book in one hand and a passport in the other. An Asian importing business led to Hollywood scriptwriting until her characters demanded their own novels. She writes romantic intrigues set in far corners of the world, including *Stinger*, available at audible.com. Diana's website is dianarchambers.com.

BILL FITZHUGH

Spicy Beans

I'm from Mississippi, a state whose historical native cuisine consists primarily of two food groups: (1) fried anything and (2) vegetables boiled with a chunk of pork fat until they've reached the consistency of pureed caterpillars. Now, don't get me wrong, I love some fried fill-in-the-blank and the taste of salty pork fat sliding down my gullet, but I also love not having quadruple bypass surgery. Call me squeamish. (Note to self: possible opening line for next novel.)

Flash forward a few years and I'm living in a small apartment in the San Fernando Valley, struggling to find work as a sitcom writer. One night at a local bar called Re$iduals (where TV residual checks for less than $1 were worth $5 at the bar) I met my future wife, Kendall.

After we dated for a while, Kendall invited me to move in to her spacious apartment in Malibu. I'll do anything for love . . . and an ocean view. So I moved.

By this point in my career, the television industry had made it abundantly clear that my services were not required, so I started to write my first novel, *Pest Control*. Since I was home all day working on the book (and not bringing home a regular paycheck) and since Kendall had a real job, we struck a deal: As long as I had dinner ready when she got home from work, she'd cover any shortages on my part of the rent.

Now, at the time, Kendall was subsisting on a macrobiotic diet, which, as far as I could tell, consisted primarily of things like small rocks and twigs poached in tap water. So while I lovingly prepared broiled soil and roasted wood chips for her, I would make, say, a pork tenderloin chop with mustard cream sauce for myself. (When I said I'd do anything for love, I meant anything short of eating things like compost.)

At any rate, it wasn't long before I noticed sniffing and lip-licking sounds coming from Kendall's direction. Finally, she asked if she could have a "just a little" of the sauce to put on her boiled pine nettles.

It was a slippery slope from there. Next she tried a bite of the chop itself. Then, quicker than you could say, "I used to be vegan," she was all, "Where the hell is *my* pork chop?" I had corrupted her.

In time we decided both diets had their merits, so we found a balance between our carnivorous desires and the healthier plant-based fare. We created what came to be known as "Rice Night." This was typically brown rice cooked with red wheat berries with edamame and a bit of tofu on the side. Eventually I came up with something a bit more substantial to top the brown rice. I called it Spicy Beans (and the recipe, like all others, is not protected by copyright, just so you know).

YIELD: 2 ENTRÉE SERVINGS, OR 3–4 SIDE DISH SERVINGS

1 or 2 tablespoons olive oil
½ cup chopped onions, shallots, or leeks
1 carrot, diced
1 celery stalk, chopped

1. Heat the oil in a saucepan over medium heat. Add the onions. Cook briefly.

2. Add the carrot and celery (for that matter, you can add chopped bell pepper or other crunchy vegetables). Cook for 5 minutes over medium heat, stirring occasionally.

3. Chop the chipotle pepper(s) and add them and their sauce to the vegetables. Cook for a few minutes, stirring now and then to spread the pepper and adobo sauce.

1 or 2 chipotle peppers in adobo sauce, depending on your tolerance for heat (La Constena brand is my favorite)

1 tomato, chopped (optional)

1 15-ounce can black beans, drained

½ cup chicken stock, divided (or water if you don't have stock, but why don't you? It's so easy to have on hand. I've never understood why, oh, never mind.)

¼ to ½ cup chopped cilantro

4. Add the tomatoes (if using) and then black beans, and stir well. Cook for a few minutes, until beans are heated through. Add ¼ cup of the stock, stir, and bring to a simmer. Cook for a few minutes.

5. Using a potato masher, mash the beans and vegetables a bit so that you end up with a consistency *approaching* the refried beans you get at a Mexican restaurant, but not quite. I like to leave some of the beans whole. If it gets too pasty, add more stock to thin it out.

6. Top with chopped cilantro and serve as a side dish or on top of brown rice (with or without red wheat berries).

Note: Leftover spicy beans make a fabulous sandwich. Toast some good bread, reheat the spicy beans, smear 'em on the bread, and top with cilantro.

BILL FITZHUGH is the award-winning author of nine satiric crime novels. The late, great humorist and political commentator Molly Ivins called Fitzhugh "A seriously funny guy." The *New York Times* said he "is in a league with Elmore Leonard and Carl Hiaasen." Fitzhugh is currently at work on his next novel.

THE LAST SUPPER

WHEN A MEDICAL EXAMINER OR CORONER PERFORMS AN AUTOPSY ON A murder victim, he is trying to determine not just the exact cause and manner of death, but the time of death as well. That can play an important role in helping the police figure out who the killer is.

To determine time of death, the ME relies on a number of factors: body temperature, rigor mortis, lividity, and stomach contents, according to D. P. Lyle, MWA member and the Edgar-nominated author of *Forensics: A Guide for Writers,* part of the Howdunit series.

"Stomach contents are very significant to an investigator," says Dr. Lyle. "Body temperature and rigor mortis can be affected by outside factors, like the temperature of the room the person died in. But the stomach empties within two to four hours no matter what else is going on." If the victim's stomach contains largely undigested food, then death probably occurred within an hour or two of the meal. If the stomach is empty, the ME knows the person probably died more than four hours after eating.

Lyle, who also pens mysteries (including *Run to Ground*), offers a hypothetical example of a traveling businessman found murdered in his hotel room. If he had dinner with a colleague from 8 to 10 p.m. and then returned to his room, the finding of a full stomach would indicate that death occurred between 10 p.m. and midnight.

"Stomach contents," says Lyle, "can support a suspect's alibi—or blow it wide open."

—Kate White

CATHY PICKENS
Fried Yellow Squash

In the South, the "three" on the menu at a "meat and three" restaurant means you choose three from a list of "vegetables" to go with your fried chicken or smothered pork chop or fried croaker or barbecue. The list would include corn and cabbage or green beans, cooked until limp, with fatback, (Suffice it to say that heart disease anywhere in your family history would make fatback a no-no for you.)

In writing about Avery Andrews, a small-town lawyer, I had to make sure she had a place to eat. Thus was Maylene's Restaurant born, a wholly imaginary place comfortably similar to countless restaurants where I've slid across cracked vinyl booths to enjoy some good eating. Because of the food pictured on my early book covers, I occasionally got e-mails that bordered on hate mail: "Where are the &*%$ recipes? What kind of mystery is this, anyway?" I didn't think recipes belonged in those books, so I started taking Avery to a few real-life restaurants, including Jestine's in Charleston for Co'Cola cake and Yesterday's in Columbia, South Carolina, for chicken-fried steak.

The highlight at any Southern meal has to be either fried okra or fried squash (battered in cornmeal or flour and deep-fried). Southern gardens produce an abundance of butter-yellow crookneck squash. When someone fries you up a batch of sweet, fresh yellow squash, you know you're loved.

Note: This recipe is very forgiving. Increase or decrease the number of squash you use, depending on who's coming for supper. Season to taste; stick your finger in the flour mixture and taste it. Some cooks dredge the squash in the flour mix, dip it in the milk, and then dredge it again before frying it.

YIELD: 2–4 SERVINGS

Oil for frying

1 to 2 eggs

½ cup milk (or buttermilk)

1 to 4 medium yellow squash, sliced into rounds about ¼ inch thick 1 cup flour

1 cup cornmeal

Salt and black pepper to taste

1. Heat about 2 inches of oil in a large Dutch oven or very large skillet. The oil has to be hot (350°F or 400°F) to cook the squash properly.

2. Layer some paper towels on a large plate and set it beside the stove.

3. Lightly beat the eggs in a bowl and add the milk. Soak the squash in the milk-egg mixture for a few minutes while you prepare the flour mixture.

4. In a bowl or large plastic bag, mix the flour, cornmeal, salt, and pepper.

5. Remove some squash from the milk mixture (enough for one layer in your Dutch oven or pot) and add to the flour mixture. Dredge or gently shake to thoroughly coat.

6. Add the squash to the hot oil in a single layer and fry until toasty brown (about 3 minutes). The oil should sizzle when you drop in a test piece.

7. Lift out the cooked squash and drain on the paper towels. Cook the remaining squash in batches and serve immediately, while hot.

Native Southerner **CATHY PICKENS** is the author of the Southern Fried mysteries (St. Martin's/Minotaur) and Charleston Mysteries walking tour (History Press). She is a past MWA board member, past president of Sisters in Crime, and president/founding board member of Charlotte's Forensic Medicine Program.

LUCY BURDETTE
Shrimp and Grits

In the process of writing the third Key West food critic mystery, *Topped Chef,* I invented a reality TV cooking contest on the island. The prize was a big deal—a shot at starring in a cooking show on national TV. (My protagonist, Hayley Snow, was pressed into judging.) When the three contestants were asked to present their "signature" seafood dishes, Randy Thompson, a proponent of homey Southern cooking, made shrimp and grits.

Most Southern cooks worth their collards have a recipe for shrimp and grits. The difference comes in several ways. First, the grits can be cooked in water, chicken broth, or milk (after which cheese and/or butter are mixed in). Then the shrimp are cooked with all or some of these ingredients: bacon, Tasso ham, onions, scallions, peppers, garlic, lemon, parsley, Worcestershire sauce, more butter. Here's my version, which Randy made for the *Topped Chef* contest. (It was a winner!)

YIELD: 4 SERVINGS

2 cups chicken broth

1 cup cornmeal grits

1 cup cheddar cheese

3 to 4 tablespoons butter, divided

6 slices bacon, chopped

1 bunch scallions, chopped

1/2 green pepper, finely chopped

Olive oil as needed

5 to 7 shrimp per person, depending on size, peeled and deveined (Randy uses Key West pinks and so do I)

1/2 lemon

1/4 cup chopped parsley

1. Bring 1 cup water and the broth to a boil, and then slowly add the grits.

2. Reduce heat to low and simmer for about 1/2 hour, whisking often to keep lumps from forming and to prevent the grits from sticking to the pan. (Take care because the grits will "pop" and can burn the cook.)

3. Mix in the cheese and 2 tablespoons of the butter, and set aside.

4. While the grits are cooking (or even earlier), fry the chopped bacon until crisp. Set this aside and pour off most of the grease from the pan.

5. Sauté the scallions and the peppers in the same pan for several minutes, adding a little olive oil if needed. Scrape the vegetables out and set them aside. Sauté the shrimp with a little olive oil or butter until barely pink (about 3 minutes).

6. Squeeze the lemon over the shrimp and add 1 tablespoon of butter. Scrape the vegetables back into the pan and warm everything together.

7. Arrange the shrimp over the grits, and garnish with parsley and bacon.

Note: This could also be served as a main course with a green salad or steamed spinach or asparagus. And biscuits if you need them.

Clinical psychologist **LUCY BURDETTE** (aka Roberta Isleib) has written twelve mysteries, including the latest in the Key West food critic series, *Murder with Ganache.* Her books and stories have been short-listed for Agatha, Anthony, and Macavity awards. She's a past president of Sisters in Crime. Read more at lucyburdette.com.

GIGI PANDIAN

Caramelized Onion Dal

As the child of cultural anthropologists from New Mexico and the southern tip of India, I grew up traveling around the world and eating many different cuisines. My travels inspired my mystery series about a globetrotting Indian American historian and also inspired my cooking. My latest novel, *Pirate Vishnu*, takes place partly in India, so I thought I'd share one of my favorite Indian recipes.

The recipe is a variation on a dish in the family cookbook my mom put together. It's a pretty basic recipe, but I love it because an accident turned it from a good dish into a heavenly one. One day I accidentally let the onion start to caramelize when I was busy with something else. When I mixed the onion with the other ingredients, the result was amazing. Jaya Jones, my protagonist in the Treasure Hunt Mystery series, would approve of the spicy and sweet flavor combination in this dish—though I expect she would also add some spicy Indian pickle.

YIELD: 4 SERVINGS AS A SIDE DISH, OR 2 AS A VEGETARIAN MAIN COURSE

1 cup yellow lentils (*toor dal* at an Indian food store; substitutions also work well: yellow split peas or red lentils)

1 teaspoon ground turmeric

1 teaspoon sea salt

½ teaspoon ground black pepper

¼ teaspoon cayenne pepper (or more to taste)

2 tablespoons olive oil

1 large onion

1 teaspoon cumin seeds

1. Rinse the lentils.

2. Add lentils to a 2-quart saucepan with 2 cups water, turmeric, salt, black pepper, and cayenne pepper. Bring to a boil. Lower the heat and simmer for 30 to 45 minutes.

3. Once the lentils are cooking, slice the onion.

4. Warm the olive oil in a skillet on medium heat and add the onion and cumin seeds. Cook the onion slowly for the duration of the time the lentils are cooking. This will caramelize the onion, bringing out its natural sugars.

5. Stir the onion mixture into the cooked lentils.

6. Serve with rice or naan. For added spice, serve with Indian pickle.

USA Today best-selling author **GIGI PANDIAN** writes the Jaya Jones Treasure Hunt mystery series (*Artifact* and *Pirate Vishnu*) and *The Accidental Alchemist*, which features a vegan chef and includes recipes. Her first novel was awarded a Malice Domestic Grant and named a "Best of 2012" debut by *Suspense Magazine*. For more, visit gigipandian.com.

LISA SCOTTOLINE

A Tomato Sauce for All Seasons

My mother thought it ain't tomato sauce unless it cooks for three days, but that's the only thing she was ever wrong about. Bottom line, I love to cook and eat but I have a life, and so do you. Listen to me and make this as your new and improved tomato sauce recipe. You won't be sorry, I promise. And with one slight variation, you can use the same recipe for winter or summer, like a jacket that's reversible, only you can eat it.

YIELD: 4 SERVINGS

3 tablespoons regular olive oil

4 average-size tomatoes, cut into thick slices

Salt and pepper to taste

A few big garlic cloves (optional)

Pecorino romano cheese (preferably Locatelli), for serving

1 sprig fresh basil, for serving

1. Pour the olive into a sauté pan and then add the tomato slices. Season with salt and pepper.

2. Cover the pan. Set the burner on medium and sauté the tomatoes until they are soft but not dead. This takes about 7 to 9 minutes. (If you like garlic, throw in a few cloves when you add the tomatoes and they'll mushify by themselves in the same period. *You don't have to do anything else.*)

3. Dump the sauce over cooked spaghetti, grate some pecorino romano, and add the sprig of fresh basil. Eat two helpings.

And in summer, forget the heat. Throw the tomatoes in a food processor. Add 3 tablespoons of olive oil and a few cloves of garlic and puree for 30 seconds. Dump it over cooked spaghetti. *You still don't have to do anything else.* Except try to stop eating at two helpings.

Mangia!

LISA SCOTTOLINE is the author of nineteen novels, including *Come Home*, and a former MWA president.

ALLISON LEOTTA

The World's Best Red Sauce
(aka Leotta Sauce)

This is an easy, quick way to make the world's best Italian red sauce. It's the Leotta family's go-to recipe and the basis for a hundred other Italian recipes. Use it as the base for homemade pizza, lasagna, or chicken parmesan. Simmer with chicken, shrimp, or meatballs to make a meat sauce. Sauté zucchini, mushrooms, or artichokes in olive oil, and then simmer in the tomatoes for a vegetarian sauce. (This is one of the few meals where my picky kids demand seconds.)

In two of my novels—*Discretion* and *Speak of the Devil*—some key scenes take place in the fictional Sergio's restaurant, which is owned by FBI agent Samantha Randazzo's family. This red sauce is always simmering in the kitchen and infuses the restaurant scenes with a delicious aroma.

Whatever you do, prepare lots of it. And be warned: once you try it, you'll never be able to eat pasta sauce from a jar again.

YIELD: 8 SERVINGS

2 large cans whole peeled tomatoes

A handful of fresh basil leaves

2 garlic cloves, chopped

2 tablespoons olive oil

2 tablespoons sugar

Pinch oregano, or to taste

Pinch dried red pepper flakes, or to taste

Salt and black pepper, to taste

1. Drain the tomatoes and then put them in a blender along with the basil and garlic. Blend until liquid but still a bit chunky.

2. Pour tomato mixture into a large pot, adding olive oil, sugar, oregano, red pepper flakes, salt, and pepper. (Don't scrimp on the sugar—it's the secret ingredient.)

3. Simmer over low heat for 10 minutes.

4. Serve over pasta.

ALLISON LEOTTA is a former federal sex-crimes prosecutor who now writes legal thrillers drawing on her experience, for which she has been dubbed "the female John Grisham." The *Washington Independent Review of Books* says her latest novel, *Speak of the Devil*, is "taut and fast-paced, . . . intelligent, probing and clear-eyed, . . . part morality tale, part riveting drama, . . . and very, very good."

BILL PRONZINI

Nameless's Italian Garlic Bread

I can't take credit for this recipe. It was concocted many years ago by my "Nameless Detective" character for a special dinner he prepared for Kerry Wade when he was trying to win her hand. She liked it so much that it helped convince her to marry him. Or so he claims, anyway.

I *can* attest to the fact that while some of Nameless's culinary inventions are suspect, this one is pretty good—his magnum opus, as it were. I've made and served it to quite a few people who enjoy real garlic bread (as opposed to the often wimpy restaurant variety) and none of them has ever refused a second offering. One friend, a very good Italian chef in his own right, has been known to eat several pieces straight out of the oven. When he comes for dinner, I have to make an extra half loaf just for him.

What to serve it with? Just about any Italian fare. It goes particularly well with antipasti, lasagna, ravioli, eggplant and chicken parmigiana, spaghetti and meatballs, and pesto dishes. *Buon appetito!*

YIELD: 1 LOAF

1 loaf French bread, preferably extra-sour sourdough

¾ cup (1½ sticks) butter

4 to 8 minced garlic cloves, depending on how much you like garlic

6 ounces shredded Parmigiano-Reggiano and/or pecorino romano cheese

Paprika

1. Preheat oven to 350°F. Slice loaf of bread in half lengthwise.

2. Melt butter and garlic together in a saucepan on low heat. Spoon mixture over bread halves, spreading evenly.

3. Cover each half with a layer of shredded cheese, and sprinkle with paprika to taste.

4. Bake uncovered on foil until cheese melts to golden brown and bread crust is crisp. Cut into 1-inch pieces and serve hot.

BILL PRONZINI has published more than eighty novels, over half of which are in his iconic Nameless Detective series, as well as four nonfiction books and 350 short stories. His most recent novels are a Nameless title, *Strangers* (Tor/Forge, 2014), and, in collaboration with Marcia Muller, *The Body Snatchers Affair* (Tor/Forge, 2015).

MEG GARDINER

The Kinsey Mill Oklahoma Biscuits

This is my grandmother's biscuit recipe. Today you can bake these biscuits on a cookie tray in a stainless-steel oven, but she grew up on the prairie, where the biscuits were cooked in a skillet in a wood-burning stove. When I was writing *The Shadow Tracer*, which opens in Oklahoma, I baked these biscuits, loaded them up with honey, and ate them hot out of the oven to help me feel like I was there on the plains. (Also because I can eat them until I fall over, but mostly to get myself in the mood to write about Oklahoma.)

YIELD: 10–12 BISCUITS

2 cups flour

2½ teaspoons baking powder

½ teaspoon salt

⅓ cup shortening

¾ cup milk

1. Preheat oven to 475°F.

2. Sift flour, baking powder, and salt into a bowl.

3. Cut in shortening with a fork or pastry cutter until the mixture resembles coarse cornmeal.

4. Add milk. Blend with a fork or pastry cutter only until the flour is moistened and the dough pulls away from the bowl.

5. Roll out dough to ¾ inch thick. Knead for 30 seconds. Cut into biscuits using a cookie cutter or the open end of a 2-inch drinking glass.

6. Bake for 12 to 15 minutes.

MEG GARDINER is a best-selling author of twelve novels, including *China Lake*, which won the 2009 Edgar Award for Best Paperback Original. Her latest novel is *Phantom Instinct*.

RHYS BOWEN

Rhys's Scone Recipe

HER ROYAL SPYNESS SHARES THE SECRET TO A PERFECT ROYAL TEA PARTY

Whether I am having tea with the queen (I'm not making this up!) or in my grandfather's humble kitchen, afternoon tea is my favorite meal. The perfect afternoon tea should include cucumber or watercress sandwiches, thin brown bread or buttered fruit bread, scones with clotted cream and jam, Victoria sponge, assorted little cakes and biscuits (preferably homemade), and of course a pot of tea.

Tea is always loose leaf, good quality. It can be Indian or Chinese. Darjeeling is a personal favorite and is served with milk. Chinese teas are lighter and scented or smoky in flavor. They are always served with lemon. Earl Grey is a black tea but flavored with bergamot, giving it a unique flavor. Always make tea with boiling water and leave at least 3 minutes before pouring. Don't allow it to sit and stew.

YIELD: ABOUT 12 SMALL SCONES

1½ cups self-rising flour, plus extra for dusting

1 teaspoon cream of tartar

½ teaspoon baking soda (also known as bicarbonate of soda)

½ teaspoon salt

3 to 4 tablespoons butter or shortening

⅔ cup milk

1. Preheat oven to 425°F. Lightly butter a baking sheet.

2. Sift together the flour, cream of tartar, baking soda, and salt into a bowl. Rub or cut in the butter until the mixture becomes large flaky crumbs. Stir to a soft dough by mixing in the milk.

3. Roll out to a thickness of ½ inch or just over, and cut into rounds with a biscuit cutter, 2 to 2½ inches in diameter. Dust with flour.

4. Arrange rounds on the baking sheet fairly close together. Bake for 12 to 15 minutes. They will rise and turn golden.

5. The scones can be served cold, but are excellent while still hot. Of course, scones are best when served with strawberry jam and clotted Devonshire or Cornish cream. (You can also add raisins, sultanas, or currants to make a fruit scone or grated sharp cheese to make a savory scone). Since it is hard to buy clotted cream in the States you can get something close to it by whipping extra heavy whipping cream until it almost turns into butter.

RHYS BOWEN is the *New York Times* best-selling author of two historical mystery series: the Molly Murphy novels, set in early 1900s New York City, and the Royal Spyness mysteries, featuring a penniless minor royal in 1930s England. Rhys's books have won fourteen major awards. Her latest book is *Queen of Hearts*.

ANGELA ZEMAN

Grappa-Soaked Cherries

Once upon a time, in a woods far away (Long Island), my husband and I joined a wine tasting group led by a doctor friend. We would dine at each other's houses for feasts matched (hopefully) to perfect wines, about which we would give opinions.

It had to happen. My night arrived. I chose to serve duck. Woe is me. You may rightfully assume this was my debut experience with duck, but I also had a good butcher's instructions, so no worries, right? First: trim the fat off the ducks. I trimmed fat. More fat. Endless fat! An impressive amount of fat!

Hang on, the sauce will get here.

The party began at seven. We started with hors d'oeuvres, I suppose, memory not being my forte. But unforgettable was the nonarrival of the duck. It roasted and roasted. I took it from the oven, poured off a *lake* of fat, returned it to continue roasting. That was at about ten p.m. I'd made other dishes, nobody fainted from starvation . . . but we were hungry.

Finally my husband said (desperate to support me), "She made a sauce for the duck; I can't wait until you try it. It's incredible."

So the doctor, captain of our group, commanded this sauce to appear. Probably out of boredom.

But one taste, and suddenly he was spooning it out of the dish directly into his mouth. He passed it on with reluctance. Around the table it went. Same result. I fetched more. *Publishers Weekly* would've given it a star. The duck continued doing whatever it was doing in the oven—certainly not cooking. My husband dove for the freezer and started dishing out ice cream. So as you now see, this sauce is flexible. That night, for us, it became our *dessert* sauce.

So this recipe, despite beginning the night intended for the entrée, instead crowned our dessert. Luscious and rich, it can be used on anything. Pork chops to venison—most kinds of meat, fish, or fowl. It can crown sponge cake, ice cream, crepes, waffles . . . so if you wish for a descriptive name, you might call this sauce "promiscuous," or "A Lady of Pleasure." We just call it *sauce*. I present: grappa-soaked cherries.

YIELD: VARIABLE

A bunch of beautiful "end of season" bright red cherries, trimmed

A large bottle of clear plain grappa (*vital: no herbs or flavorings*)

Sugar, to taste (The issue here is that you are making as much sauce as you want, so you must add sugar in a

1. Slice the cherries in half and remove the pits, trying not to damage the fruit. They must look pretty for the party. (As pretty as possible. Aiming for perfection will spoil your life.)

2. Pick out any old ugly cherries and throw them away.

3. Put about ½ inch of water into a pan, and set on a burner over medium-low heat. In a few minutes, pour the grappa liquid into the water. Continue to heat.

4. Add sugar and stir until it is melted. Then taste. Does it need more sugar? More water? (Don't try this on an empty stomach.) At each addition of sugar, let the mixture cook to melt the sugar. Cook down

relative amount. Just remember, it's easy to add more but a real problem to remove if you used too much. So add it to the pan in small amounts, tasting as you go.)

Water (I bet you knew that was coming. Not much. Hold that aside, you may or may not need it, according to taste.)

Frangelico liqueur (just a smidgen)

the liquid a bit, until the sauce gains some body. By "body" I mean a viscous texture. You don't want hard candy, but you don't want red water either. To play with the texture (not taste), add water.

5. When you think the sauce tastes right and has a nice viscous body, add a bit of Frangelico. Not a lot. You don't want to put in so much that you change the taste of the sauce. You want to just "influence" the taste. It's a secret!

6. Next to the last step: Gently add the lovely fresh cherries. Transfer to a nice sauceboat, if you have one. Present it to your guests with its partner for the evening—whether it's veal roast or waffles. Serve warm.

7. Last step: Whip off that apron. Bow.

ANGELA ZEMAN claims wit never dies in her stories, but other life-forms must fend for themselves. Her work is published by Otto Penzler, AHMM, and others. Her website is angelazeman.com.

CHAPTER SIX

"But you see, it must have been the sherry, dear." Mrs. Pennington set aside ~~the~~ her knitting and reached for the teapot. "Who would poison a perfectly good homemade cake?"

JOSEPH FINDER

Doreen's Apple Crumble

Whenever anyone calls Twitter a big waste of time, I always point out that it is thanks to Twitter that I ended up with the perfect recipe for what the Brits call apple crumble (and we call apple crisp)—something so simple that I can make it even when I'm distracted by a book deadline and that reliably comes out so good that people always ask for the recipe. But until now I've never given it out.

I got it from an English woman I "met" through Twitter named Rosanne Kirk (@RosieCosy). It's an old family recipe she got from her mother, Doreen Kenny. (I've tweaked it a bit.) I forget why Rosie sent it to me. I must have tweeted a picture of one of the apple trees at our house on Cape Cod (we grow, if you care, Macouns and Honeycrisps and Gravensteins), and I think she asked what I was planning to do with all those apples. Later I (nonvirtually) met Rosie and her mom at the crime writing festival in Harrogate, in the United Kingdom.

Rosie asked me not to give this recipe out to anyone else, and for years I kept it under seal, to the annoyance of numerous dinner guests. But now Rosie's given me official clearance to declassify it, so here it is . . . Notice there are no rolled oats in this recipe. Oats in apple crumble are an abomination. The Brits serve this with custard sometimes, but I think vanilla ice cream is the way.

YIELD: 4–6 SERVINGS

- ½ cup (1 stick) unsalted butter, cut into small pieces
- 8 ounces (2 cups) self-rising flour (it'll come out OK if you use plain old all-purpose flour)
- ½ cup brown sugar (demerara if you can find it)
- 6 large apples, peeled, cored, and sliced around ½ inch thick
- 3 tablespoons sugar (or less, depending on how tart your apples are)
- 1 teaspoon ground cinnamon (optional)
- 1 teaspoon vanilla extract

1. Preheat the oven to 350°F and position a rack in the center of the oven. Spray the bottom and sides of a 9-inch square glass baking dish with cooking spray. (Or butter it. Also no big deal if you have only an 8-by-8-inch casserole dish or individual serving dishes.)

2. Rub or cut the butter into the flour until the mixture resembles bread crumbs. You can use a pastry cutter—or a food processor for a few quick seconds. Mix in the brown sugar. Put the whole mix into the freezer while you do the next step.

3. Put the apples in a mixing bowl and add the granulated sugar. Sprinkle the cinnamon over the apples, add the vanilla extract, and put the apples in the prepared baking dish. Remove the crumble mixture from the freezer and sprinkle it over the apples.

4. Bake for about 45 minutes, or until you can see the juice of the apples coming through the topping and the topping itself is golden brown.

JOSEPH FINDER is the *New York Times* best-selling author of eleven suspense novels, including *Paranoia*, the basis for the Harrison Ford/Gary Oldman movie; and *High Crimes*, the basis for the Morgan Freeman/Ashley Judd movie. His novels have won awards from the Strand Magazine Critics and the International Thriller Writers. His latest is *Suspicion* (Dutton). He lives with his family in Boston.

SHEILA CONNOLLY

Apple Goodie

When I first started planning the Orchard Mysteries, I knew what the setting would be—a creaky 1760 colonial farmhouse in a rural New England town. The house came first: it was built by one of my ancestors, and I've prowled the attic and the basement and what's left of the original hundred or so acres of land, so I know it inside and out.

But an old house wasn't enough to carry a cozy mystery series, so I started thinking about what I could add—and the answer was apples. Every colonial home had an orchard, for pie and eating apples and dried apples and cider (yes, even hard cider) and vinegar for preserving. We've all grown up with stories of Johnny Appleseed (a very distant cousin of mine) and mottos like "An apple a day keeps the doctor away." Apples strike a chord with almost everyone, so what could be better?

I've been making this recipe since long before I started writing. It comes from the mother of a college friend, and she gave it the name Apple Goodie. It's easy to make and it tastes good—everything a dessert should be. It's my all-time favorite comfort food.

YIELD: 4 GENEROUS SERVINGS, OR 6 SKIMPY SERVINGS

4 cups cored, peeled, and sliced apples (a variety that softens without turning into mush—Granny Smiths work well)

¾ cup granulated sugar

1 tablespoon flour

½ teaspoon ground cinnamon

TOPPING

½ cup rolled oats

½ cup brown sugar

½ cup flour

Pinch salt

¼ cup (½ stick) butter

⅛ teaspoon baking soda

½ teaspoon baking powder

1. Preheat the oven to 375°F.

2. Grease a 2-quart casserole or similar dish (the shape doesn't really matter).

3. Toss the apples with the sugar, flour, and cinnamon, and place in the greased dish.

4. Mix the topping ingredients together to make coarse crumbs (you can use your hands) and sprinkle them over the apples.

5. Bake for 35 to 40 minutes until the topping is brown and bubbly.

6. Serve warm or at room temperature. You may add whipped cream or ice cream—but you don't have to!

New York Times best-selling author **SHEILA CONNOLLY** has been nominated for Anthony and Agatha awards. She currently writes three cozy mystery series for Berkley Prime Crime, and her e-books *Relatively Dead*, a paranormal romance, and *Reunion with Death*, were published in 2013. Her most recent book is *Razing the Dead*.

GAYLE LYNDS

The Hungry Spy's Deep-Fried Chocolate Bananas

Take off your trench coat, step into the kitchen, and turn off your smartphone. You're about to create a thrilling dessert, and you won't want even an urgent call from the director of Central Intelligence to interrupt you.

YIELD: 6 SERVINGS

12 ounces high-quality dark chocolate

A sprinkle of sea salt, preferably from someplace exotic like Timbuktu

2 pounds firm, medium-ripe bananas

Oil for frying

1 cup cake flour

1 cup heavy cream

1 cup pulverized bread crumbs

Powdered sugar

1. Melt the chocolate in a double boiler. Remove from the heat, stir in the salt, and set aside to cool.

2. Peel the bananas and slice them into cylinders 3 inches long. Use an apple corer to core the bananas, and cut or break the cores into smaller pieces. Plug one end of each banana cylinder with a small piece of core.

3. Stand the banana cylinders on the plugged ends. Pour the melted chocolate into a squeeze bottle and squeeze the chocolate into the empty centers of the bananas. Then plug the open end of each cylinder with another piece of core. Put the bananas in the freezer.

4. Ten minutes before cooking, remove the bananas in the freezer and start heating the oil to 400°F.

5. Put the cake flour, heavy cream, and bread crumbs each into a separate shallow bowl. Roll the bananas in the flour, then dredge them in the heavy cream, and finally dredge them in the bread crumbs.

6. Fry the bananas in the oil until golden brown. Sprinkle with powdered sugar and enjoy.

New York Times best seller **GAYLE LYNDS** is the award-winning author of a dozen international espionage novels including *Assassins* and *The Book of Spies*. *Publishers Weekly* lists her book *Masquerade* among the top ten spy thrillers of all time. She's a member of the Association of Former Intelligence Officers. Visit her at gaylelynds.com.

JACQUELINE WINSPEAR

Syllabub

I think I loved the idea of syllabub long before I ever experienced the taste of this lemony, creamy, sherry-laden pudding. It was probably the word *syllabub* itself—it seems to come in waves across the tongue (I think I like the idea of acquiring a Catahoula hound for the same reason. And I love the city name Jalalabad—I think it's those *ls*.). Syllabub is an old English pudding—and it bears saying that it soothes my sense of nostalgia that the word *pudding* is back in fashion again. Many trendy London restaurants have of late dispensed with using *dessert* in favor of the more traditional *pudding* or *afters*.

True syllabub requires time and patience, plus knowing how to scald cream and whisk a mixture containing egg whites until it is firm but not curdled—though in Elizabethan times curdling was required, because the mixture was later strained. Many recipes specify wine, but I prefer cream sherry or another fortified wine or "sack" such as Madeira. But for those who have not rolled up their sleeves to make a good syllabub before, here is an easy recipe—without the egg whites and with measurements given in simple old-fashioned half-pints and spoonfuls, and with the odd cup for American readers.

This is clearly not a recipe for the cholesterol-challenged, but lovely if you want to indulge.

Finally, a word on nutmeg for all mystery fans—and this gleaned from the doctor I worked for as a receptionist when I was in college. Nutmeg is considered a poison with no really effective antidote in an overdose situation, so always be careful with that particular spice—don't drop it on the floor for the Catahoula hound to find. Use sparingly. Unless you want to kill someone.

Here goes!

YIELD: 6–8 SERVINGS, DEPENDING ON THE SIZE OF YOUR GLASSES

½ pint scalded cream*
(ideally heavy or
"double" cream)

½ pint unscalded cream

1 tablespoon sifted fine
granulated sugar

About 1 cup (8 ounces)
cream sherry

4 tablespoons brandy

A little grated nutmeg

Juice of 1½ lemons

1. Whisk everything together until the mixture is nice and frothy with little "peaks" and pour into wine glasses.

2. Chill for at least 3 hours, and serve.

Note: Here's something that looks nice: Finely grate some lemon rind before you juice the lemons, and then sprinkle just a little of the grated rind on top of each glass of syllabub before serving. My absolute favorite is to put sliced almonds on top, to give a bit of a crunch—especially if you've browned them in saucepan with a dab of butter first. And chocolate lovers will adore syllabub topped with shaved dark chocolate—oh, yum!

*A word on scalding cream: "Scald" means to heat to just under the boiling point. You don't want to burn it, so if this is the first time you've done something like this, use a double boiler, or put the cream into a small bowl and then set the bowl on a saucepan of boiling water. (You only need an inch of water in the pan, and make sure you choose a pan that the bowl can sit on comfortably. It's hard to get it just right, but as long as the steam heats up the cream, you're in business.) Of course it's easy to put the cream straight into a pan on a low heat, but do keep stirring and be vigilant to avoid burning. In fact, this latter method gives the cream a sort of caramel-ish flavor.

JACQUELINE WINSPEAR is a *New York Times* best-selling author known for her series featuring World War I nurse turned psychologist-investigator Maisie Dobbs, as well as the 2014 stand-alone best seller, *The Care and Management of Lies*. Originally from the United Kingdom, Jacqueline lives in California.

POE WAXES POETIC ON FOOD

EDGAR ALLAN POE IS CONSIDERED THE INVENTOR OF DETECTIVE FICTION, AND though his stories are dark and terrifying, he clearly found joy in a good meal. The proof is in the following excerpt from a letter written to his mother-in-law in 1844. According to Christopher Semtner, curator of the Edgar Allan Poe Museum in Richmond, Virginia, Poe was moving from Philadelphia to New York and was in the process of looking for another publisher.

"Poe might have been especially pleased with his meal because he did not always eat well," explains Semtner. "At times when he was running out of money, his mother-in-law would have to make a stew from whatever she could afford. There are stories of her carrying a pot to relatives' homes to beg for scraps from them during lean times."

New York, Sunday Morning April 7—just after breakfast.

My Dear Muddy,

We have just this minute done breakfast, and I now sit down to write you about everything. …Last night, for supper, we had the nicest tea you ever drank, strong & hot—wheat bread & rye bread—cheese—tea-cakes (elegant) a great dish (2 dishes) of elegant ham, and 2 of cold veal piled up like a mountain and large slices—3 dishes of the cakes and, and every thing in the greatest profusion. No fear of starving here. The landlady seemed as if she couldn't press us enough, and we were at home directly. . . , For breakfast we had excellent-flavored coffe, hot & strong—not very clear & no great deal of cream—veal cutlets, elegant ham & eggs & nice bread and butter. I never sat down to a more plentiful or a nicer breakfast. I wish you could have seen the eggs—and the great dishes of meat. I ate the first hearty breakfast I have eaten since I left our little home.

—**Kate White**

DIANE MOTT DAVIDSON

Fa-La-La Fruitcake Cookies

I first encountered a version of this recipe at a cookie exchange over three decades ago. I thought it had possibilities and started experimenting. Our family and friends loved the final version so much that I now make many dozens every year. The dough keeps well, and the cookies keep fabulously in an airtight tin.

YIELD: 8 DOZEN

1½ cups (3 sticks) unsalted butter, room temperature

3 cups firmly packed dark brown sugar

3 large eggs, room temperature

¾ cup buttermilk

5¼ cups all-purpose flour

1½ teaspoons baking soda

1½ teaspoons kosher salt

3 cups candied cherries, quartered (use both red and green for festive color)

3 cups chopped dates

1. In the large bowl of an electric mixer, beat the butter on medium speed until it is very creamy, 2 to 4 minutes.

2. Add the brown sugar and beat very well until the mixture is light and fluffy.

3. Add the eggs one at a time, beating well after each addition; stir in the buttermilk.

4. Sift the dry ingredients. Using a wooden spoon, stir the dry ingredients into the mixture until no flour can be seen.

5. Stir in the chopped cherries and dates.

6. Cover the bowl with plastic wrap and refrigerate for 24 hours.

7. When you are ready to make the cookies, remove the bowl from the refrigerator and allow the dough to soften slightly, about 10 minutes.

8. Preheat the oven to 375°F. Butter a cookie sheet or line it with a silicone mat.

9. Using a 1½-tablespoon ice cream scoop, scoop out the dough and place each piece 2 inches apart on the sheet.

10. Bake for 12 to 16 minutes, rotating the cookie sheet halfway through the baking time. The cookies will turn golden brown and will not look like batter, and, when touched lightly, almost no imprint will remain.

11. Cool the cookies on racks. When the cookies are completely cool, store them in zip-top plastic bags (which you can freeze) or in airtight containers.

New York Times best-selling author **DIANE MOTT DAVIDSON** has published seventeen mysteries featuring caterer-sleuth Goldy Schulz. The series began with *Catering to Nobody* (1990), followed by *Dying for Chocolate* (1992), and, most recently, *The Whole Enchilada* (2013). She has received the Anthony Award and *Romantic Times'* Best Amateur Sleuth Novel award.

WILLIAM BURTON McCORMICK

Latvian Solstice Squares

I was introduced to these wonderful dessert squares while I living in Riga, the capital and largest city of Latvia, to research my novels. At the height of summer it is tradition in Latvia to head to the countryside to celebrate the solstice with communal cookouts, bonfire jumping, and midnight mass skinny-dipping (all meant to cleanse the soul). During breaks from these festivities I became addicted to the wonderful square snacks that were common around our campsite. It took me years to track down the recipe and approximate the ingredient mixtures for Western tastes, but I hope the daring among you will take a "bite of the Baltic" and enjoy these scrumptious delights.

YIELD: 50 SQUARES

½ cup melted butter or margarine

1 package German chocolate cake mix (alternately coconut pecan cake mix or golden chocolate chip cake mix may be used)

6 ounces semisweet chocolate chips

6 ounces peanut butter chips

6 ounces butterscotch chips

6 ounces almond brickle chips

½ cup chopped nuts

14 ounces sweetened condensed milk

1. Preheat oven to 350°F.

2. Grease a 9-by-13-inch rectangular pan.

3. In a medium bowl, use a fork to stir butter into cake mix. Resulting dough will be very stiff.

4. Using a rubber spatula, pour dough evenly into the greased pan.

5. Layer chocolate chips, peanut butter chips, butterscotch chips, almond brickle chips, and nuts evenly over the dough.

6. Pour sweetened condensed milk over the top.

7. Bake for 30 minutes or until golden brown and bubbly.

8. Cool completely on a wire rack.

9. Cut into 1½-inch squares.

WILLIAM BURTON McCORMICK lived for three years in Latvia and Russia to write his first novel, *Lenin's Harem*, a historical thriller about the Red Riflemen of the Bolshevik Revolution. A two-time Derringer finalist, his fiction has appeared in most major mystery magazines. He was elected a Hawthornden Writing Fellow in 2013.

LAURIE R. KING

Mrs. Hudson's Coffee Sheet Cookies

This is the ideal recipe for a group; potluck suppers, planning meetings, teachers' luncheons—and oh, how clearly its smell shouts love when the family comes home! My mother used to make them, but secretly I believe she got the recipe from Mrs. Hudson (formerly of the aptly named Baker Street, later moved to the Sussex Downs) because any housekeeper for Sherlock Holmes had to be an expert in comfort food . . .

This can be made with decaf coffee or with another liquid entirely, such as hot apple juice. You can also substitute dried cranberries, chopped apricots, etc., for the raisins. However, the coffee/raisin/cinnamon mixture is classic for a good reason. Also, just because it makes three dozen 2-inch squares doesn't mean it will be sufficient for thirty-six individuals. Especially if it's cut into larger pieces and treated as a warm cake topped with ice cream.

YIELD: ABOUT 3 DOZEN

COOKIES
1 cup raisins
2/3 cup hot coffee
1/2 teaspoon ground cinnamon
2/3 cup softened shortening or butter
1 cup brown sugar
2 eggs
1 1/2 cups flour
1/2 teaspoon baking soda
1/2 teaspoon baking powder
1/4 teaspoon salt

GLAZE
1 cup sifted powdered sugar
Enough warm coffee to make a thin glaze

1. Preheat oven to 350°F. Grease a 10-by-15-inch jelly roll pan (a baking sheet with sides).

2. Combine raisins, hot coffee, and cinnamon in a heatproof bowl and let cool.

3. While the mixture cools, cream together shortening and brown sugar and then beat in eggs.

4. Sift together the dry ingredients. In alternating additions, stir the dry mixture and the coffee mixture into the shortening mixture. Spread evenly into the jelly roll pan. Bake for 20 to 25 minutes.

5. Remove from oven and, while hot, beat together the powdered sugar with enough warm coffee to make a thin glaze, and spread over the hot cookies. Cut into squares. Good luck trying to convince everyone that the cookies need to be cool before they're cut!

LAURIE R. KING is the best-selling author of twenty-two novels, including *The Beekeeper's Apprentice* (which the Independent Mystery Booksellers Association called "one of the 20th century's best crime novels"). She has won or been nominated for prizes from Agatha to Wolfe, was named guest of honor at several crime conventions, and has two children who survived her cooking.

JOHN LUTZ

Gooey Butter Cake
(A St. Louis Original)

Here's how it happened: In the 1930s a mistake was made by a recently hired baker at one of St. Louis's many excellent bakeries. He reached for a "smear" of deep butter, the kind used in making deep butter cakes, and accidentally came away with "gooey butter," a substance used primarily as a culinary adhesive. Rather than throw away the mistakenly made product (this being the Great Depression), the baker sold the cakes. They were so popular that he baked and sold more. And so was born the infamous (for its calories) but delicious (for everything else about it) gooey butter cake.

There are other accounts of the source of gooey butter cake, but this seems to me to be the most likely.

And it's the one I like the most.

YIELD: 12 SQUARES

1 box yellow pudding-in-mix cake mix

3 eggs, divided

½ cup (1 stick) butter, room temperature

1 1-pound box powdered sugar, divided

1 8-ounce package cream cheese

1. Preheat the oven to 350°F. Mix the cake mix, one of the eggs, and the butter until crumbly.

2. Press into the bottom of a 9-by-13-inch baking pan.

3. Blend three-quarters of the box of sugar (save the rest for topping), the cream cheese, and the other 2 eggs until creamy. Pour over the pressed mixture.

4. Bake for 30 minutes or until golden brown. Let cool slightly and then press the remaining powdered sugar into the cake.

New York Times and *USA Today* best seller **JOHN LUTZ** is the author of more than forty-five novels and 250 short stories and articles. His awards include the Edgar, Shamus, Short Mystery Fiction Society's Golden Derringer Award, and Trophee 813 Award. He is past president of both Mystery Writers of America and Private Eye Writers of America.

LINDA STASI

Mystery Baker:
Original New York City Cheesecake

Ever wonder where New York City cheesecake originated? Well, the mystery is solved.

No matter what anyone tells you, the truth is that it was invented at a restaurant called Ratner's in 1905. The restaurant was a Jewish kosher dairy joint (no meat or fowl) on the Lower East Side of Manhattan that kept dishing up the goods until 2004. Yes, ninety-nine delicious years!

So, Ratner's had a baker, a family guy who liked to think outside the cookie box. One day he combined some of the good dairy products he had on hand, like cream cheese and sour cream, and poured it into a crust of graham crackers, butter, and nuts.

When the baker passed he *literally* passed on this secret recipe to his family—who passed it on to me thirty years ago.

The good news? I didn't have to die to pass it along, although it is to die for!

YIELD: 1 9-INCH CAKE (8–10 SERVINGS)

14 to 16 graham crackers

1 to 1½ sticks melted sweet butter

½ cup chopped walnuts

4 eggs

3 8-ounce packages cream cheese

1 cup granulated sugar

¼ teaspoon almond extract

16 ounces sour cream

1. Preheat oven to 375°F.

2. Crush graham crackers and combine with 1 stick melted butter (add more if needed for moistness) and walnuts. Press the graham cracker mixture into the bottom and up the sides of a 9-inch springform pan.

3. Beat together eggs, cream cheese, sugar, and almond extract. When the mixture is lump free, blend in sour cream and beat well. Pour into the pan.

4. Bake for around 45 minutes (probably longer, but just until the cake is firm to the touch). Turn off the heat, crack the oven door, and let cake sit for 20 minutes at least. Then move it to the counter and let cool.

5. Refrigerate for at least 8 hours before serving.

Note: If desired, top the cheesecake with a single gorgeous strawberry or with fresh blueberries. Also good: In a pot combine a package of frozen berries with sugar and a tiny bit of water if needed. Boil the mixture over medium heat until it becomes jellied. Let cool a bit, and then spread over the top of the cheesecake.

LINDA STASI, an award-winning columnist for the *New York Daily News*, was a 2014 Edgar Award nominee for her first novel, *The Sixth Station*, now also available in paperback and audio. Stasi has been an on-camera cohost with Mark Simone on NY1 TV's *What a Week!* for the past twelve years.

JAMES PATTERSON

Grandma's Killer Chocolate Cake

Here's one "killer" Alex Cross always loves to catch—Grandma's Killer Cake! A special family recipe dating from the 1940s, this decadent cake seems to get better with age; it is tastier on day two. And you need to be a good detective around the house after it has been made, sitting there in its glass-domed cake stand, staring back at you with deadly temptation, because a piece seems to mysteriously disappear every time I go into the kitchen. Not to be caught red-handed, so looms the "Killer Cake Killer"!

YIELD: 1 SINGLE-LAYER 9-BY-12 INCH CAKE OR 1 DOUBLE LAYER 9-INCH CAKE

CAKE

²/₃ cup butter

2 cups granulated sugar

2 eggs

2 cups flour

1¹/₃ cups buttermilk

1¹/₃ teaspoons baking soda dissolved in ²/₅ cup hot water

3¹/₂ squares bitter chocolate, melted gently

1 teaspoon vanilla extract

FROSTING

¹/₂ cup butter

3 squares bitter chocolate

2 cups granulated sugar

²/₃ cup milk

1 teaspoon vanilla extract

1 teaspoon almond extract

1. Preheat oven to 350°F. Cream butter and sugar together. Add eggs.

2. Blend in flour and buttermilk in alternating additions, starting and ending with the flour. Add baking soda mixture, followed by chocolate and vanilla extract.

3. Pour batter into one 9-by-12-inch pan or two round 9-inch springform pans. Bake for 30 minutes, or until a toothpick inserted into the center comes out clean. Remove from oven and let cool.

4. Combine all frosting ingredients in a saucepan, bring to a full boil, and boil for 2 minutes. Let cool. You can put saucepan on ice if necessary to cool quickly.

5. Remove the cake from the pan, frost, and serve.

JAMES PATTERSON has sold 300 million books worldwide, including the Alex Cross, Michael Bennett, Women's Murder Club, Maximum Ride, and Middle School series. He supports getting kids reading through scholarships, Book Bucks programs, book donations, and his website, readkiddoread.com. He lives in Palm Beach with his wife, Sue, and his son, Jack.

MARY JANE CLARK

Sinfully Delicious Siesta Key Lime Pie

Though a Jersey girl, I spend quite a bit of time in Sarasota, Florida, specifically on Siesta Key. I've written two books that take place there (*Nobody Knows* and *Footprints in the Sand*) because the location provides so many fascinating possibilities for suspense and mystery. Plus, it's always more fun to write about things and places you love.

My various research and pleasure trips to the Suncoast have led me to experience the delights of key lime pie. It's probably my favorite dessert. In fact, my friends and I sample the key lime pie at each of the restaurants we patronize and actually rate every bite's smoothness, creaminess, tartness, sweetness, and general ability to make you close your eyes, smile, or even moan with pleasure.

In my opinion, this easy recipe for key lime pie stands up with the best of them. I make it often for friends. My characters ate it in *Footprints in the Sand*. They adored it. I hope you will, too. As you see, this is not a complicated, gourmet-style recipe, but it seems that everyone who samples this pie raves and wants more.

YIELD: 8 SERVINGS

1 8-ounce bar cream cheese (softened)

1 14-ounce can sweetened condensed milk

2 teaspoons vanilla extract

½ cup key lime juice (not regular lime juice, *key* lime juice)

1 8-inch graham cracker crust pie shell (store bought is fine)

1. With an electric mixer, beat cream cheese until creamy.

2. Gradually add sweetened condensed milk and beat until smooth. Mix in vanilla extract. Add key lime juice and blend thoroughly.

3. Pour mixture into pie shell, cover, and refrigerate for at least 6 hours.

New York Times best-selling author **MARY JANE CLARK** is the author of sixteen mystery and suspense novels. Her twelve KEY News media thrillers were inspired by her years at CBS News. *That Old Black Magic* is the fourth novel in her Piper Donovan/Wedding Cake mystery series. Mary Jane's books are published in twenty-three languages.

SHARON FIFFER

A Pan, a Plan, and a Flan

Several years ago I purchased a like-new vintage Nordic Ware yellow flan pan at an estate sale. Attending estate sales, garage sales, and flea markets is something I do in the name of research for my Jane Wheel, PPI (picker/private investigator), novels of course. I loved the pan for its yellow color and for the fact that it had a flan recipe printed on the bottom. I hung it in my yellow kitchen as art.

Needing a dessert for an impromptu dinner party, I decided to try the recipe. Or at least make up a recipe similar and see if the pan—and the basic plan for this "flan"—were worth keeping.

I replaced lemon extract with lemon zest and substituted the cream I had for the milk that I did not. I rarely use cake flour, so I used all-purpose. Once the flan was baked, I knew it was too plain to serve as dessert for company. It was a large fragrant shortbread cookie. So I spread a jar of lemon curd on top. Then I arranged fresh raspberries over that and sprinkled it with a little powdered sugar.

No lemon curd? Jam plus fresh fruit and whipped cream would work. Even goat cheese and figs, if you wanted to go savory. This is the little black dress of desserts. Accessorize accordingly.

Note: This is English flan, not a flan de leche or a caramel custard. This recipe makes more of a buttery cake or a shortbread. It can be baked in a tart pan or 8- to 9-inch shallow cake pan.

YIELD: 6–8 SERVINGS

¼ cup (½ stick) butter

¾ cup granulated sugar

3 egg yolks

1¼ cups flour (sifted cake flour if you're a stickler)

2 teaspoons baking powder

½ teaspoon salt

Zest of 1 lemon, or ½ teaspoon lemon extract (or both if you like it lemony)

½ cup cream, milk, or half-and-half

1 10-ounce jar lemon curd

½ to 1 pint fresh raspberries, blackberries, or blueberries

1. Preheat oven to 350°F. Grease and flour a tart pan or an 8- or 9-inch cake pan.

2. Beat butter, sugar, and egg yolks until fluffy. Sift (or stir) together dry ingredients; add to butter mixture alternating with lemon zest and cream; blend well. Pour into prepared pan.

3. Bake for about 25 minutes, or until a toothpick inserted into the center comes out clean. Let cool completely, and then remove cake carefully from pan. If you've used a tart pan or a vintage Nordic Ware flan pan (see above!), you'll have an indentation on the top, which will really help you with the next step. But if your cake is flat, it will still work deliciously, although perhaps not as beautifully.

4. Spread the top with lemon curd and arrange raspberries artfully. Refrigerate for at least an hour.

SHARON FIFFER is the author of eight "stuff" mysteries published by St. Martins/Minotaur featuring antiques picker, junker, and private investigator Jane Wheel; the most recent title is *Lucky Stuff*. Fiffer, like her heroine, collects vintage kitchenalia, recipes, cookware, and kitsch—strictly for research purposes.

RITA LAKIN

Lemon Poppy Seed Sponge Cake

My folks moved from New York to Florida years ago, when I moved to California. I visited them often and I was inspired to write a comedy novel about their lives in wacky Fort Lauderdale, a place where silliness was a way of life. I based my books on my retired mother, my aunts, and their friends, turning them into over-the-hill detectives. (Picture them in a car chase; the killers are driving 90 mph, Gladdy is doing a steady 35.) The first in the series was entitled *Getting Old Is Murder* and the latest, number seven, is *Getting Old Can Kill You.*

This family recipe comes from Gladdy Gold and her merry band of adorable senior lady private eyes, whose agency motto is "Never trust anyone under 75." Of course, "the girls" eat most meals at Moe's deli for the early bird dinner special (3:00 right on time; 4:30 fugedaboudit, too late, the kasha varnishkes are gone by then). But nobody makes a lemon poppy seed sponge cake better than their very own Ida.

This recipe takes maybe fifteen minutes, give or take a few, depending on age and mobility. (And if you forgot to heat the oven, then you have to wait again for it to heat.)

YIELD: 12 SERVINGS, OR 6 IF YOUR GUESTS HAVE A GOOD APPETITE

½ cup poppy seeds

½ cup boiled milk (nonfat preferred)

1½ cups (3 sticks) butter (low calorie, of course)

1½ cups granulated sugar (or Splenda), divided

2 teaspoons grated lemon rind

2 teaspoons grated orange rind

8 eggs (from cage-free hens), separated

Dash salt

¾ teaspoon cream of tartar

1. Grease and flour a 10-inch Bundt pan and preheat oven to 350°F.

2. Soak poppy seeds in milk for 5 minutes.

3. Blend butter, 1¼ cups of the sugar, lemon and orange rind, and egg yolks. Add flour and salt, and gently mix. Drain poppy seeds and set aside; discard milk.

4. In a separate bowl, beat egg whites until stiff as a board. Fold in the remaining ¼ cup sugar, cream of tartar, and poppy seeds. Fold this into batter and pour into prepared pan. That's it. Easy peasy.

5. Bake for 50 to 60 minutes until done. Serve warm with herb tea or decaf coffee (for those under doctor's orders). Enjoy, read, and eat.

RITA LAKIN worked for twenty-five years in television as a writer and a producer. Her credits include *Dr. Kildare*, *Peyton Place*, *Mod Squad*, and *Dynasty*. She has written seven comedy mystery novels about Gladdy Gold and her senior group of private eyes. She won Left Coast Crime Lefty Award in 2009 for *Getting Old Is a Disaster*. Her many nominations and awards include the Writers Guild of America Award, the MWA Edgar Award, and the Hopwood Award from the University of Michigan. Visit her website: ritalakin.com.

LOIS LAVRISA

Cozy Southern Chocolate Chip Pudding Cake

My cozy mystery series, which is set in beautiful historic Savannah, Georgia, involves "The Chubby Chicks Club" (who are neither all chubby nor all chicks). Bezu, the Southern belle of the club, makes muffins for her boarders, including a version based on this cake. A little warning: If you are a boarder of Bezu's, you may not make it out alive. Bezu's muffins are delicious and will not kill you, but watch out for the other tenants, who may have it in for you.

YIELD: ABOUT 12 SERVINGS

About ½ stick butter, for pan

¼ cup flour, for pan

1 box yellow moist cake mix (any brand)

1 5¼-ounce package instant vanilla pudding (any brand)

4 eggs (medium or large)

1 11½-ounce bag milk chocolate chips or semi-sweet chocolate chips

½ cup vegetable oil

½ cup milk (whole or 2%)

1¼ cups sour cream

1. Preheat the oven to 350°F. Rub the inside of a Bundt pan with a thin coating of butter, add flour, and shake around until the flour is stuck on the butter. Then tap out any leftover flour. Or spray the pan with baking spray that contains flour.

2. Mix remaining ingredients in a mixing bowl with a fork until moist. Using a spatula, pour mixture into the prepared Bundt pan. Bake for 60 minutes.

3. Let cool for about 2 hours. Then tip Bundt pan upside down on a plate (the cake should slide out easily since you greased and floured the pan).

Optional serving suggestions: Sprinkle powdered sugar on top, and/or serve with a scoop of vanilla ice cream.

LOIS LAVRISA's *Liquid Lies* was recognized as finalist in the 2013 Eric Hoffer Award. The first book in her new cozy mystery series, *Dying for Dinner Rolls*, became an Amazon Kindle top 100 bestseller and earned her a nomination for 2014 Georgia Author of the Year. Her latest is book two in the series, *Murderous Muffins*.

WENDY CORSI STAUB

Ho Ho Ho and a Bottle of Rum

My mom made the most amazing rum cake. It was moist, coated in a sugary glaze and caramelized nuts. She had a heavy hand when it came to pouring the rum, so everyone felt extra merry after a couple of slices (I dare you to stop at just one!).

I got the recipe from her a few years back, before she passed away, and began making the cake every December. It started small—just one cake, which I'd make and serve when we had holiday company. But it drew such praise that I started making them for people. And when I sent one over to my publishing house the week before Christmas, the rave reviews from those who had managed to snag a piece before it disappeared were so enthusiastic that I had to send three more so that everyone could try it—along with the recipe. A tradition was born.

These days, I've collected enough Bundt pans to make eight rum cakes at a time. I send several to my current and backlist publishing houses and to various other colleagues (when I met the gang at Carol Fitzgerald's Bookreporter offices in person, I was introduced as "Wendy—you know, Rum Cake Wendy"). Since I can't send one to all of you, I'm giving you the recipe. Enjoy!

YIELD: 1 BUNDT CAKE

CAKE

1 cup chopped toasted pecans

1 18½-ounce box yellow cake mix

1 1¾-ounce box instant vanilla pudding mix

4 eggs

½ cup cold milk

½ cup vegetable oil

½ cup Barcardi dark rum

GLAZE

½ cup (1 stick) butter

¼ cup water

1 cup granulated sugar

½ cup Barcardi light rum or coconut rum

1. Preheat oven to 325°F. Grease and flour a 12-cup Bundt pan. Sprinkle nuts on bottom of pan.

2. Combine all remaining cake ingredients. Beat for 2 minutes with an electric mixer on high speed.

3. Pour batter into prepared pan. Bake for 1 hour. Let cool in pan.

4. Invert onto a serving plate. Prick the top of the cake with a fork.

5. Make the glaze: Melt butter in a saucepan. Stir in water and sugar. Boil for 5 minutes, stirring constantly. Remove from heat and stir in rum.

6. Drizzle glaze over cake. Use a pastry brush or a spoon to scoop up the extra drippings and pour it back on the cake.

Note: My secret is to use another half recipe of the glaze so that the cake is extra moist—in other words, I make it with 1½ sticks butter, ¼ cup plus 2 tablespoons water, 1½ cups sugar, and ¾ cup light rum. Then, instead of drizzling it over the cake, I use a marinade injector (looks like a large syringe!) to inject it into the cake.

Two-time finalist for the Mary Higgins Clark Award, **WENDY CORSI STAUB** has published nearly eighty novels, including multiple *New York Times* best sellers. Her latest, *The Perfect Stranger*, follows *The Good Sister*, one of *Suspense Magazine*'s "Best of 2013." The trilogy concludes with *The Black Widow*.

CHAPTER SEVEN

We know the suspect had motive. We know he had cyanide. But how did he poison just <u>one</u> glass of punch?

ALISON GAYLIN

The "Smoking Gun" Margarita

I was living in a small Mexican mountain town when I started writing my first book, *Hide Your Eyes*. Years later, after moving back to the States, that town still haunted me—its narrow cobblestone streets, its looming colonial buildings with their colorful doors and gargoyle-shaped gutters, so bright and cheerful during the day but at night cloaked in shadows and mystery. It had such potential for suspense that I wound up setting my fourth book, *Heartless*, in the fictional Mexican village of San Esteban.

To this day, I still associate Mexico with writing. So when I finally hit the *USA Today* best-seller list with my fifth book, *And She Was*, and our dear friends Jamie and Doug Barthel threw me a party, they very appropriately chose a Mexican theme.

The margarita they served—refreshing, but with a smoky heat that lingers—has since become my celebration drink of choice.

YIELD: 4 DRINKS	
Margarita salt (if desired)	1. Rim four glasses with margarita salt, if desired. Place glasses in the fridge or freezer.
1 jalapeño pepper, sliced	2. Place the jalapeños in a microwave-safe bowl, pour 3 ounces of the tequila over them, and microwave for 10 seconds.
12 ounces tequila (Hornitos or Herradura are my favorites, but any brand is fine), divided	3. Ignite the jalapeños and let them burn briefly.
4 cups crushed ice	4. Fill a blender with the ice. Add the liquid ingredients and then the jalapeños. Blend well at high speed.
4 ounces Cointreau	5. Serve in the chilled glasses. Enjoy!
8 ounces fresh lime juice	

USA Today and internationally best-selling author **ALISON GAYLIN** received an Edgar nomination for her first book, *Hide Your Eyes*. Her Shamus Award–winning novel, *And She Was*, was also nominated for the Thriller, Anthony, and RT awards. Her eighth book is *Stay with Me*—the third in the Brenna Spector series (HarperCollins).

NERO WOLFE
ON FOOD

IN EVERY ONE OF THE SEVENTY-THREE MYSTERIES BY REX STOUT, THE rotund and irascible protagonist Nero Wolfe sits down in his home with fellow detective Archie Goodwin to an incredible meal served by the butler, Fritz. When it comes to food in the Manhattan brownstone, no expense is spared. Caviar is mixed in with breakfast eggs; figs are flown in from Chile in winter.

Here, cooking advice from the great gourmand and brilliant detective:

"Shucked and boiled in water, sweet corn is edible and nutritious; roasted in the husk in the hottest possible oven for forty minutes, shucked at the table, and buttered and salted, nothing else, it is ambrosia. No chef's ingenuity and imagination have ever created a finer dish."

"Chili is one of the great peasant foods. It is one of the few contributions America has made to world cuisine. Eaten with corn bread, sweet onion, sour cream, it contains all five of the elements deemed essential by the sages of the Orient: sweet, sour, salty, pungent, and bitter."

"Do you know shish kebab? I have had it in Turkey. Marinate thin slices of lamb for several hours in red wine and spices . . . thyme, mace, peppercorns, garlic . . ."

"You don't mix salad dressing in the kitchen. You do it at the table and use it immediately."

—Kate White

JUSTIN SCOTT AKA PAUL GARRISON

Captain Will's High Latitudes Vodka Gimlet

Most sailors are tinkerers, particularly in the interest of creature comfort. This terrific vodka gimlet on the rocks has been tinkered with twice. Ironically, both improvements were developed ashore, but it will travel. (If you're not way far north or south, you'll have to hail a vessel with an ice maker or make sail for the nearest marina.)

Hard-pressed bartenders at the Yale Club of New York City pioneered a technique to slow the inevitable watering down of drinks served on the rocks. They mix the drink in a cocktail shaker filled with ice, as they would if pouring it straight up. But instead they serve it in a capacious old-fashioned glass full of fresh ice.

A hundred miles to the north-northeast, meanwhile, at the Mayflower Inn in the quiet Litchfield Hills, bartenders with more time on their hands have subtly modified the traditional gimlet's ingredients. They go easy on the Rose's Lime Juice and squeeze in fresh lemon and fresh lime. Combined, these two improvements yield an arrestingly crisp, cold cocktail worthy of the name High Latitudes Vodka Gimlet.

YIELD: 2 SERVINGS

6 ounces vodka

2 teaspoons Rose's Lime Juice

Juice of ½ lemon

Juice of ½ lime

Thin lime wedge or thin shaving of lemon peel, for garnish

1. Fill a cocktail shaker two-thirds full of ice. Add ingredients. Shake 33 times. (The 33-shakes technique was developed Down East in the sea-farers' town of Portland, Maine. It works because it reminds us that the exquisite cannot be rushed.)

2. Pour into old-fashioned glasses full of fresh ice or serve straight up in chilled stem glasses.

3. Garnish with a thin wedge of lime or a thin shaving of lemon peel—Captain Will's preference.

JUSTIN SCOTT's *The Shipkiller* is among the ITW's *Thrillers: 100 Must-Reads*. Twice nominated for the Edgar, Scott writes the Ben Abbott mysteries, the Isaac Bell adventure series with Clive Cussler, and—under his Paul Garrison pen name—modern sea stories and Robert Ludlum "Janson" thrillers. *The Assassin*, with Clive Cussler, debuts in 2015.

PETER JAMES

The Peter James
Vodka Martini Writing Special

This is my 6 p.m. tipple, which acts as my rocket fuel to kick off my evening's writing. One sip of this, music blasting from my speakers, and I'm typing away happy as Larry!

YIELD: SERVES 1 AUTHOR!

Grey Goose vodka (or your preferred brand; this is mine)

Martini Extra Dry vermouth

1 thin 3-inch strip lemon rind plus 1 lemon wedge, or 4 plain olives, pitted

1. Fill a cocktail shaker halfway with ice cubes.

2. Fill a proper crystal martini glass of decent quality (no other drinking vessel can be substituted!) three-quarters full of vodka.

3. Using the cap of the Martini Extra Dry bottle, measure 2 capfuls of vermouth and add to the glass.

4. Pour contents of the glass into the shaker and secure the top carefully.

5. Now you have a choice: a twist or olives. My taste alternates!

WITH A TWIST:
Drop the lemon rind into the glass. Make an opening in the center of the lemon wedge and run it all the way around the rim of the glass on both sides.

WITH OLIVES:
Spear the olives with a cocktail stick and place in the glass.

6. Give the cocktail shaker a hard shake, remove the cap, and pour the drink into the glass.

Enjoy! But remember the caveat: "Ladies and gents, beware the dry martini, have two at the very most . . . for with three you will be under the table . . . and with four you will be under your host."

PETER JAMES is the author of twenty-five thrillers. His seven consecutive Sunday *Times* number one best-selling Roy Grace crime novels are published in thirty-six languages with sales of over fourteen million copies. They have also been number one best sellers in France, Germany, Spain, Russia, and Canada. His latest novel is *Want You Dead*.

GARY PHILLIPS

The Switchblade Cocktail

This cocktail was created by mixologist Jackie Patterson Brenner. It was to celebrate the launch of a line of hard-boiled books, the Switchblade imprint, which Andrea Gibbons and I edited for PM Press. It premiered with a reprint of my novel *The Jook*, about a wayward pro football player, and Summer Brenner's (Jackie's mother-in-law) rugged original *I-5* about sex trafficking. While the imprint is no more, thankfully the cocktail endures.

I have one or two Switchblades, while puffing on a maduro-type cigar, each time I polish off a deadline . . . or sometimes when after-hours rolls around.

YIELD: 1 DRINK	Stir ingredients with ice until properly diluted and well chilled. Garnish with grenadine.
2 ounces Martin Miller's gin	
¾ ounce Dolin Blanc vermouth	
1 bar spoon Luxardo maraschino liqueur	
2 dashes St. George Spirits absinthe	
Dash Small Hands Foods grenadine, to garnish	

GARY PHILLIPS draws on his experiences ranging from running a shadowy political action committee, to teaching incarcerated youth, to delivering dog cages in writing his tales of chicanery and malfeasance. His latest work includes the graphic novel *Big Water* and the Nate Hollis private eye short stories. His website is gdphillips.com.

CHUCK GREAVES

The Hard Twist

Before I was a novelist, and before I was a lawyer, I was a Fire Island bartender intent on perfecting the ultimate in summer beverages, one of which I've rechristened for this cookbook. This recipe is perfect for a sunny cocktail party or barbecue. Although Jack MacTaggart—my lawyer/detective series character—would prefer a cold Budweiser to any cocktail whose recipe includes the word *garnish*, even Jack would have to admit that it's a fabulous thirst-quencher after a hot day solving crime.

YIELD: 1 DRINK

1 tablespoon Campari

¼ cup freshly squeezed red grapefruit juice

6 tablespoons tonic water

1 red grapefruit slice, for garnish

Fill a tumbler with ice. Shake Campari, grapefruit juice, and tonic together in a cocktail shaker. Pour drink into tumbler and garnish with grapefruit slice.

CHUCK GREAVES, who was a New York bartender before attending law school, now authors the award-winning Jack MacTaggart series of legal mysteries. *The Last Heir* (Minotaur), a wine-country whodunnit, is the latest installment. To learn more, visit chuckgreaves.com.

TINA WHITTLE

Chatham Artillery Punch

My series protagonist, Tai Randolph, may run a Confederate-themed gun shop in Atlanta, but her heart remains in Savannah, Georgia, her hometown. When Tai worked there as a River Street tour guide, she enjoyed telling stories about the vengeful ghosts, star crossed lovers, and battle-weary soldiers of this moss-draped, marsh-scented port city.

The Civil War is woven deeply into the Low Country's mythology, as is one of Savannah's most infamous libations—Chatham Artillery Punch. Artillery punch traces its origins to the Chatham Artillery unit, a standing militia for Chatham County, Georgia, formed in 1785. The artillery was also a social organization, with soirees and cotillions featured prominently in its social calendar. But no matter how innocently the party punch started out, when the gentlemen secretly added their favorite spirits to the bowl, it would take a decidedly dangerous turn.

The punch's best-known moment came during December 1864, however, when General William Tecumseh Sherman marched his troops upon Savannah. Despite the swath of scorched destruction he left behind, Sherman didn't burn Savannah. According to legend, he was so enchanted with the hospitality of the Low Country ladies that he spared the city from the torch. Was artillery punch part of a clever Southern strategy to distract and conquer? Or was Sherman's decision one of purely martial strategy? Only the live oaks and cobblestones know the truth. And they're holding that secret close.

YIELD: 20 SERVINGS

1 lemon, sliced thin

1 lime, sliced thin

1 orange, sliced thin

½ cup brown sugar, packed

⅔ cup rum

2 cups sweet red wine

2 cups brewed black tea

½ cup orange juice

¼ cup lemon juice

½ cup bourbon

⅓ cup cognac

⅓ cup brandy

1 bottle Champagne or sparkling wine

1. Place the lemon, lime, and orange slices in a 1-gallon zip-top food storage bag; add the brown sugar and rum and marinate in the refrigerator overnight (up to 3 days is acceptable).

2. At serving time, stir together the red wine, tea, orange juice, lemon juice, bourbon, cognac, and brandy in a large punch bowl until well combined. Add the marinated fruit slices.

3. Just before serving, add the Champagne. Add crushed ice to your preference (the more ice, the less potent the punch). Enjoy in respectful moderation—this libation has laid low some of the mightiest.

TINA WHITTLE's Tai Randolph/Trey Seaver series—featuring intrepid gun shop owner Tai and her corporate security agent partner Trey—has garnered starred reviews in *Kirkus*, *Publishers Weekly*, *Booklist*, and *Library Journal*. The latest *Deeper Than the Grave* (Poisoned Pen Press). Learn more at tinawhittle.com.

DEANNA RAYBOURN

March Wassail Punch

Drinking wassail is an ancient tradition. Dating back to Saxon times, the word comes from the greeting "wæs hæl," roughly translated as "be you healthy." In the counties of southern England renowned for cider production, drinking wassail originated as a bit of sympathetic magic to protect and encourage the apple trees to bear fruit. While wassail and other punches were very popular during Regency times, by the later part of the nineteenth century they had been largely supplanted by wines and other spirits. My characters the Marches, however, care much more for their own pleasure than for what is fashionable. They serve their wassail the old-fashioned way, out of an enormous wooden bowl mounted in silver with a roasted apple garnish. Their wassail is, as tradition dictates, served quite hot and is deceptively alcoholic. Proceed with caution.

YIELD: 6 SERVINGS FOR MARCHES, OR 10 FOR ORDINARY FOLK

Approximately 1 cup brown sugar

12 small apples, cored

2 pints hard cider (see note)

4 cinnamon sticks (or substitute ½ teaspoon ground cinnamon), plus extra for garnish

About 3 whole cloves (or substitute ¼ teaspoon ground cloves)

Fresh ginger and fresh nutmeg to taste

1. Preheat oven to 350°F. Loosely spoon brown sugar into the cavity of each apple and place apples in a casserole dish with a small amount of water. Bake until tender, plump, and bursting from their skins, approximately 45 minutes to an hour, depending on the size of the apples.

2. Meanwhile, gently warm the cider in a large pot over low heat. Grind whole cinnamon and cloves with a mortar and pestle and combine (or combine store-bought ground cinnamon and cloves). Add spices to the warming cider and continue to warm slowly until hot but not boiling.

3. Grate in fresh ginger and fresh nutmeg to taste. (Lord March's secret ingredient is a cup of his very best port, added just in time to heat through.)

4. To serve, place an apple in a heatproof punch glass and ladle the wassail over top. The March family recipe calls for a garnish of a fresh cinnamon stick for each glass. Slice any remaining apples for garnish, if desired. Extra roasted apples are also delicious with cream, yogurt, or ice cream.

Note: Hard cider is not available in the juice aisle of the grocery store. It is wonderfully alcoholic and tastes deeply of apples. You can find bottled varieties at wine and liquor stores, but the very best is fermented by apple farmers for their own use. Find one and befriend him. The Marches get their cider at the source from the Home Farm at Bellmont Abbey.

New York Times best-selling novelist **DEANNA RAYBOURN** is a sixth-generation native Texan with a degree in English and history. Her novels have been nominated for numerous awards including five RITAs, two RT Reviewers' Choice awards, the Agatha, two Dilys Winns, a Last Laugh, and three du Mauriers.

BETH AMOS
Holiday Grogg

This warm, spicy drink is one that amateur sleuth Mack Dalton (of *Murder on the Rocks* and *Murder with a Twist*, which I wrote as Allyson K. Abbott) would keep simmering in her bar during the holidays . . . though this heady mix of smells and flavors might make her synesthesia go crazy! It's the perfect accompaniment for holiday get-togethers and a tasty warmer to enjoy in front of a roaring fire after a cold day of sledding or other outdoor activities. It appeals to adults and children alike (leave out the rum for the kids). Mix it up in minutes and leave it to simmer all day long in your slow cooker with a ladle beside it, so people can help themselves. It has the added benefit of making your house smell wonderful!

For parties, I double the recipe, put half in the fridge and half in the slow cooker, and just add more to the cooker as needed throughout the party.

YIELD: 8–10 SERVINGS, DEPENDING ON THE SIZE OF THE MUGS

1 quart apple cider

1 quart cranberry juice

2 cups orange juice

¾ cup brown sugar (light or dark)

2 teaspoons ground cinnamon

6 mandarin oranges

12 whole cloves, or 1 teaspoon ground cloves

Dark rum (optional)

Cinnamon sticks

1. Combine all the juices in a slow cooker. Add brown sugar and cinnamon and stir well to mix.

2. Slice the mandarin oranges in half and push 2 cloves into the peel side of each half (this is optional; you can also just toss the cloves into the juice, but doing it this way adds the flavor without leaving little clove pieces floating around that might end up in drinks). Add to the slow cooker. If you are using ground cloves, just stir it into the juice mixture.

3. Heat on high until steaming, then lower heat and let simmer for as long as you want, stirring periodically.

4. To make individual drinks, ladle some of the liquid into a mug (leave the mandarin oranges in the pot), add 1 ounce of dark rum if desired, and top off with a cinnamon stick.

5. At the end of the day, the mix can be cooled and refrigerated overnight and then reheated the following day. The flavor just gets better!

Best-selling author **BETH AMOS** (bethamos.com) writes mysteries under the pseudonyms Annelise Ryan and Allyson K. Abbott. *Murder with a Twist*, the second in the Mack's Bar series (Abbott), came out in August 2014. Her latest is *Stiff Penalty*, book six in the Mattie Winston series (Ryan).

LAURA CHILDS

Killer Sweet Tea

In steamy Charleston, South Carolina, where my series character Theodosia Browning presides over the Indigo Tea Shop, tea reigns supreme. Time slows down, tea drinking is elevated to a genteel art, and the aroma of fruity Darjeelings, malty Assams, and toasty Keemuns fills the air and imparts an almost aromatherapeutic effect. But murder lurks in the cobblestone alleys and narrow carriageways that thread through Charleston's historic district. And two-century-old feuds still rear their ugly heads. They say revenge is a dish best served cold. So is this Southern sweet tea!

YIELD: 1 PITCHER

3 cups water for boiling

3 tea bags (black tea or flavored)

¾ cup granulated sugar

6 cups cold water

1. Bring 3 cups of water to a boil in a saucepan. Add tea bags. Simmer for 2 minutes and then remove from heat. Cover and let steep for 10 minutes.

2. Remove tea bags and add sugar, stirring until dissolved. Pour into a 1-gallon jar or pitcher. Add the cold water and ice cubes. Enjoy!

LAURA CHILDS is the *New York Times* best-selling author of the Tea Shop Mysteries, Scrapbooking Mysteries, and Cackleberry Club Mysteries. Her most recent books are *Steeped in Evil* and *Gossamer Ghost*. Previously, Laura was CEO of her own marketing firm, authored several screenplays, and produced a reality show.

LEE CHILD

Coffee, Pot of One

OK, this ain't exactly rocket surgery, but as always it helps to pay attention. Use a standard mid-range drip machine, nothing expensive, but nothing too cheap, either. Cuisinart works for me, with a gold-colored mesh filter seasoned by a couple months' hard use. First, fill the jug with water, and then tip the jug into the machine. If you want to get fancy you can use bottled water, because city water's chlorine content ain't your friend with this endeavor. Evian works well. For every little number on the side of the jug, subtract one and use that many spoons of ground coffee. Anything from Colombia will do. Or if you're flush, try Jamaica Blue Mountain coffee. Avoid any kind of flavoring or other adulteration. Close the lid, hit the switch, wait five, and you're there.

But choose your mug carefully. Bone china is ideal, fine and translucent if you can get it, tall, narrow, cylindrical in section. Avoid a thick rim and avoid heavy stoneware. The rim needs to feel like a blade against your lips, and any kind of weight or thickness in the cup will leach heat out of the drink too fast. And avoid any kind of dairy product or sweetener, obviously. This is coffee we're making here, not some syrupy milk drink.

Born in England, **LEE CHILD** now lives in New York City and leaves the island of Manhattan only when required to by forces beyond his control. For information on the Jack Reacher novels and more, visit Lee online at leechild.com.

METRIC CONVERSIONS

Use these rounded equivalents to convert between the traditional American systems used to measure volume and weight and the metric system.

VOLUME

AMERICAN	IMPERIAL	METRIC
¼ teaspoon		1.25 milliliters
½ teaspoon		2.5 milliliters
1 teaspoon		5 milliliters
1 tablespoon		15 milliliters
¼ cup (4 tablespoons)	2 fluid ounces	60 milliliters
⅓ cup (5 tablespoons)	2½ fluid ounces	75 milliliters
½ cup (8 tablespoons)	4 fluid ounces	125 milliliters
⅔ cup (10 tablespoons)	5 fluid ounces	150 milliliters
¾ cup (12 tablespoons)	6 fluid ounces	175 milliliters
1 cup (16 tablespoons)	8 fluid ounces	250 milliliters
1¼ cups	10 fluid ounces	300 milliliters
1½ cups	12 fluid ounces	355 milliliters
1 pint (2 cups)	16 fluid ounces	500 milliliters

WEIGHTS

AMERICAN	METRIC	AMERICAN	METRIC
¼ ounce	7 grams	8 ounces (½ pound)	225 grams
½ ounce	15 grams	9 ounces	250 grams
1 ounce	30 grams	10 ounces	280 grams
2 ounces	55 grams	11 ounces	310 grams
3 ounces	85 grams	12 ounces (¾ pound)	340 grams
4 ounces (¼ pound)	110 grams	13 ounces	370 grams
5 ounces	140 grams	14 ounces	400 grams
6 ounces	170 grams	15 ounces	425 grams
7 ounces	200 grams	16 ounces (1 pound)	450 grams

INDEX

ABOUT MWA

Mystery Writers of America is the premier organization for mystery writers, professionals allied to the crime writing field, aspiring crime writers, and those who are devoted to the genre. MWA is dedicated to promoting higher regard for crime writing and recognition and respect for those who write within the genre. It provides scholarships for writers, sponsors MWA:Reads (its youth literacy program, formerly known as Kids Love a Mystery), sponsors symposia and conferences, presents the Edgar® Awards, and conducts other activities to further a better appreciation and higher regard for crime writing.

TH AMOS ⇒—● KATHLEEN ANTRIM ●—⇒ CONNIE ARCHER ☠ FRANKIE Y. BAILEY

USAN M. BOYER ☠ SANDRA BROWN ⇒—● LESLIE BUDEWITZ ●—⇒ CAROLE BUGGÉ

☠ DIANA CHAMBERS ●—⇒ JOELLE CHARBONNEAU ⇒—● LEE CHILD ☠ LAUR

LAN COBEN ⇒—● NANCY J. COHEN ●—⇒ KATE COLLINS ☠ MAX ALLAN COLLINS AND

HERINE COULTER ☠ DIANE MOTT DAVIDSON ⇒—● NELSON DeMILLE ⇒—● GERAL

M FAY ●—⇒ LYNDSAY FAYE ☠ SHARON FIFFER ⇒—● JOSEPH FINDER ●—⇒ BILL FIT

RYL WOOD GERBER ⇒—● SUE GRAFTON ●—⇒ CHUCK GREAVES ⇒—● BETH GROUNDWA

DY HORNSBY ●—⇒ DAVID HOUSEWRIGHT ☠ PETER JAMES ⇒—● J. A. JANCE ⇒

ISON LEOTTA ☠ LAURA LIPPMAN ⇒—● KEN LUDWIG ●—⇒ JOHN LUTZ ⇒—● GAYL

JOHN McEVOY ⇒—● BRAD MELTZER ●—⇒ DAVID MORRELL ⇒—● MARCIA MULLER ●—⇒

JAMES PATTERSON ☠ CHRIS PAVONE ⇒—● LOUISE PENNY ●—⇒ TWIST PHELAN

●—⇒ KATHY REICHS ●—⇒ BARBARA ROSS ☠ LAURA JOH ROWLAND ⇒—● S. J.

J. SELLERS ⇒—● KARIN SLAUGHTER ●—⇒ LINDA STASI ⇒—● WENDY CORSI STAUB

KATE WHITE ⇒—● TINA WHITTLE ●—⇒ JACQUELINE WINSPEAR ⇒—● BEN H. WINT

NKIE Y. BAILEY ●—⇒ ADRIENNE BARBEAU ⇒—● RAYMOND BENSON ●—⇒ KARNA SMALL

AROLE BUGGÉ ☠ LUCY BURDETTE ⇒—● ALAFAIR BURKE ●—⇒ LORENZO CARCATERR

LAURA CHILDS ⇒—● C. HOPE CLARK ☠ MARY HIGGINS CLARK ⇒—● MARY JANE CLAR

BARBARA COLLINS ●—⇒ SHEILA CONNOLLY ⇒—● THOMAS H. COOK ☠ MARY ANN C

ERALD ELIAS ⇒—● J. T. ELLISON ☠ DIANNE EMLEY ⇒—● HALLIE EPHRON ●—⇒ LIN

BILL FITZHUGH ●—⇒ GILLIAN FLYNN ⇒—● FELIX FRANCIS ☠ MEG GARDINER ⇒

H GROUNDWATER ⇒—● KAREN HARPER ●—⇒ CHARLAINE HARRIS ☠ CAROLYN HA

A. JANCE ●—⇒ TAMMY KAEHLER ⇒—● LAURIE R. KING ●—⇒ LISA KING ⇒—● RITA

N LUTZ ●—⇒ GAYLE LYNDS ⇒—● MARGARET MARON ●—⇒ EDITH MAXWELL ☠ W

ARCIA MULLER ☠ ALAN ORLOFF ⇒—● KATHERINE HALL PAGE ⇒—● GIGI PANDIA

WIST PHELAN ⇒—● GARY PHILLIPS ☠ CATHY PICKENS ⇒—● BILL PRONZINI

S. J. ROZAN ☠ HANK PHILLIPPI RYAN ⇒—● JUSTIN SCOTT ⇒—● LISA SCOTTOLINI